Create Your Own Japanese Garden
Japanische Gartengestaltung

Japanisches Gartenforschungsinstitut

Vorwort

Es ist wohl nicht nötig zu betonen, daß japanische Gärten rund um den Globus als Gartengestaltungskunstwerke bekannt sind. Beflügelt von der natürlichen Schönheit der japanischen Landschaft und dem Wunsch, damit eine Einheit zu bilden, geht der japanische Garten weiter und versucht, eine Einheit zwischen Mensch und Natur zu schaffen.

Wenn man auf die tausendjährige Geschichte japanischer Gärten zurückblickt, gleicht keine Periode der anderen. Der japanische Garten wurde schon immer von der Kultur und den jeweiligen Bedürfnissen beeinflußt und veränderte somit sein Aussehen auf vielfältige Weise. Das seit über dreißig Jahren bestehende Japanische Gartenforschungsinstitut erkundete viele alte Meisterwerke, indem sogar teilweise Gärten abgetragen wurden, um den „Geist der Schönheit" richtig verstehen zu können. Was wir in jedem Fall dabei gelernt haben ist, daß hinter jedem dieser Meisterstücke ein Künstler mit ungewöhnlichem Geschick steckt, der Können und außergewöhnlich große Anstrengungen in sein Werk gesteckt hat.

Viele Menschen in Übersee leben in dem Glauben, daß japanische Gärten immer gleich aussehen, doch in Wirklichkeit ist die Gartenbaukunst eine sehr freie Kunstform. Japanische Landschaftsdesigner schöpfen alle Ausdrucksformen aus, um die Schönheit einer eigenen Welt zu erschaffen – das Hauptziel eines jeden japanischen Gartens.

Anläßlich des dreißigsten Geburtstags des Japanischen Gartenforschungsinstituts haben wir dieses Buch veröffentlicht, in dem die Arbeiten der vier bedeutendsten Landschaftsarchitekten japanischer Gartenbaukunst vorgestellt werden.

Die hier vorgestellten Gärten zeigen alle traditionelle Elemente und versuchen, neue Erkenntnisse zu gewinnen beziehungsweise einen Platz reinster Schönheit darzustellen.

Darüber hinaus sind diese Gärten von riesengroß bis ganz klein (ungefähr 6 x 12 Fuß) gezeigt.

Wir sind der Meinung, eine Sammlung von ganz besonderen Arbeiten zusammengestellt zu haben, die sowohl Originalität als auch die Stärke des Künstlers widerspiegelt.

Das Buch „Japanische Gartengestaltung" ist eine Sammlung, die nicht nur die stylistische Seite japanischer Gärten zeigt, sondern auch die künftigen Möglichkeiten dieser Kunstform darlegt. Wir glauben, daß es nicht nur Anregungen gibt für Leute, die ihren eigenen japanischen Garten bauen möchten, vielmehr wird es einen Standard für diejenigen vorgeben, die diese Gärten kreieren.

13. Februar 1995
Japanisches Gartenforschungsinstitut

Preface

One hardly needs to point out that the Japanese garden is recognized around the world as an achievement in the art of gardening. Deriving from the natural beauty of the Japanese landscape, and being in harmony with it, the Japanese garden goes a step further, seeking to be the ideal human dwelling place.

Looking back over the thousand year history of the Japanese garden, one never saw a period with a unified style. The Japanese garden has always been influenced by culture and the demands of the times, changing its appearance and shape in many ways.

The Japanese Garden Research Institute has been in existence for over thirty years, studying many old garden masterpieces, sometimes excavating sites, and all along learning about what is called "the spirit of beauty." What we have definitely learned is that behind the birth of every great garden is an artist of unusual compassion and strength, who puts extraordinary effort and guidance into the creation of his work.

Overseas there are many people under the impression that the Japanese garden is of a certain shape, but the truth is that it is a very free form of art. On a certain level, Japanese landscape artists will use their abilities to explore all forms of expression to create beauty of another world—the crowning achievement of the Japanese garden.

In commemoration of the 30th anniversary of the Association, we have published this book, in which the works of four garden landscapers are studied, and the various aesthetic aspects of the modern Japanese garden are particularly given attention to.

The works introduced here all show traditional principles, and yet seek to express something new, or to create a place of pure spatial beauty. Moreover, these gardens range in sizes from very large to only two tsubo (approximately 6 x 12 ft.).

Modesty aside, we feel we have managed to gather together a collection of works which demonstrate both the originality and strength of the artist's feelings.

In one sense, this book is about the message of beauty through the works of these four artists. "Create Your Own Japanese Garden," in its broadest sense, is a collection of works designed to show not only the stylistic breadth of Japanese gardens, but the future possibilities for this form of art, as well. We believe it will not only provide ideas for people simply wishing to build their own Japanese garden, but will also set a standard for those working within that world.

February 13, 1995
Japanese Garden Research Association

INHALT

Vorwort	2

Arbeiten von Isao Yoshikawa

Yubata kagetsu-tei Inn	Innengarten: Westseite	8
	Innengarten: Ostseite	10
	Vorgarten	12
Hamasei Hisago-an Restaurant		
	Vorgarten	14
	Kishin-tei Garten	16
Dairen-ji Tempel	Vorgarten	18
	Innengarten	20
Seisho-in Tempel	Nordgarten der Tempelzuflucht	22
	Nordgarten der Empfangshalle	24
	Südgarten der Priester-Wohnräume	26
Tozen-ji Tempel	Südgarten der Tempelzuflucht	27
	Vorgarten der *Shingyo* Halle	28
Komyo-ji Tempel Garten		30
Tsurugaoka Hachiman-gu Schrein,	Vorgarten der Empfangshalle	32
Shuei-ji Tempel	kleiner Garten der Empfangshalle	34
Der Shindo Home Garten		36
Iwai Home	Hauptgarten	40
	Vorgarten	43
Der Enomoto Home Garten		44
Der Iwata Home Garten		47
Der Watanabe Home Garten		50
Yakazu Home	Innengarten	53
	Klinikgarten	54
Onishi-machi Suirei-tei Garten		56

Arbeiten von Kazuo Mitsuhashi

Der Kato Home Garten	58
Der Kurosawa Home Garten	62
Der Sakai Home Garten	65
Der Ogura Home Garten	68
Kashima Home Garten	72
Der Kishimoto Home Garten	74

Chosho-ji Tempel	Garten seitlich der Haupthalle	76
	Innengarten	78
Der Ito Home Garten		80
Der Kondo Home Garten		82
Der Hanajima Home Garten		84

Arbeiten von Sabro Sone

Tenryu-ji Tempel Vorgarten		88
Nagaoka Zen-Juku Privatschule	Innen- und Vorgarten	90
Zensho-ji Tempel	Hauptgarten Vorgarten	94
Garten der Shinnyo-do Halle		95
Der Mori Home Garten		98
Der Kumagai Home Garten		102
Jomyo-ji Tempel Garten		104
Meigetsu-in Tempel	*Shumisen* Garten	106
	hinterer Garten	108
Soan-ji Tempel Garten		110
Garten des Isobe Hotels	Teichgarten	113
	Karesansui Garten	115

Arbeiten von Shin'ichi Kosuge

Der Sasaki Home Garten	118
Der Okano Home Garten	122
Der Iizumi Home Garten	125
Garten des Nishi-no-Dai Clubhaus	128
Der Takahashi Home Garten	131

Glossar	134

Wasserkörper	11
Schildkröteninsel	37
Gartenelemente	43
Gartenthemen	55
Stützmauern	63
Gartenplanung	67
Trockenes Flußbett	70
Steinarrangement	77
Bambuszaun	87

CONTENTS

Preface —————————————————————————— 3

Works by Isao Yoshikawa
Yubata Kagetsu-tei Inn; Inner garden: West side —— 8
　　　　　　　　　　　Inner garden: East side —— 10
　　　　　　　　　　　Front garden —— 12
Hamasei Hisago-an Restaurant; Front garden —— 14
　　　　　　　　　　　　　　Kishin-tei garden —— 16
Dairen-ji Temple; Front garden —— 18
　　　　　　　　Inner garden —— 20
Seisho-in Temple; Northern garden of the temple sanctuary —— 22
　　　　　　　　Northern garden of the reception room —— 24
　　　　　　　　Southern garden of the priest's living quarters —— 26
Tozen-ji Temple; Southern garden of the temple sanctuary —— 27
　　　　　　　Front garden of Shingyo hall —— 28
Komyo-ji Temple Garden —— 30
Tsurugaoka Hachiman-gu Shrine; Front garden of the reception room —— 32
Shuei-ji Temple; Small garden of the reception hall & Inner garden —— 34
The Shindo Home Garden —— 36
The Iwai Home; Main garden —— 40
　　　　　　Front garden —— 43
The Enomoto Home Garden —— 44
The Iwata Home Garden —— 47
The Watanabe Home Garden —— 50
The Yakazu Home; Indoor garden —— 53
　　　　　　　Clinic garden —— 54
Onishi-machi Suirei-tei Garden —— 56

Works by Kazuo Mitsuhashi
The Kato Home Garden —— 58
The Kurosawa Home Garden —— 62

The Sakai Home Garden —— 65
The Ogura Home Garden —— 68
Home Garden in Kashima —— 72
The Kishimoto Home Garden —— 74
Chosho-ji Temple; Side garden of the main hall —— 76
　　　　　　　Inner garden —— 78
The Ito Home Garden —— 80
The Kondo Home Garden —— 82
The Hanajima Home Garden —— 84

Works by Saburo Sone
Tenryu-ji Temple Front Garden —— 88
Nagaoka Zen-Juku Private School; Inner garden & Front garden —— 90
Zensho-ji Temple; Main garden —— 92
　　　　　　　Front garden —— 94
Shinnyo-do Hall Garden —— 95
The Mori Home Garden —— 98
The Kumagai Home Garden —— 102
Jomyo-ji Temple Garden —— 104
Meigetsu-in Temple; *Shumisen* Garden —— 106
　　　　　　　　The rear garden —— 108
Soan-ji Temple Garden —— 110
Hotel Isobe Garden; Pond garden —— 113
　　　　　　　　Karesansui garden —— 115

Works by Shin'ichi Kosuge
The Sasaki Home Garden —— 118
The Okano Home Garden —— 122
The Iizumi Home Garden —— 125
Nishi-no-Dai Clubhouse Garden —— 128
The Takahashi Home Garden —— 131

Glossary —————————————————————————— 140

Water Bank —— 11
On Turtle Islands —— 39
Reinforcing Walls —— 63
When Planning a Garden··· —— 67
Dry Streambeds —— 70
Stone Arrangements —— 77
Bamboo Fences —— 85
Garden Themes —— 96
Garden Elements —— 110

Create Your Own Japanese Garden
© Japanese Garden Research Association

Translation into English: Jay Thomas
                            Scott Brause
Translation into German: Andrea Güthaus/WEBER & WEBER

Design & Layout: Kenichi Yanagawa

All rights reserved. No part of this publication may be reproduced
or used in any form or by any means-graphic, electronic, or mechanical,
including photocopying, recording, taping, or information storage
and retrieval systems – without written premission of the publisher.

Alle Rechte sind vorbehalten. Diese Ausgabe oder Teile dieser Ausgabe
dürfen nicht vervielfältigt oder in irgendeiner Form graphisch,
elektronisch oder mechanisch verwendet werden. Photokopieren,
Aufzeichnen, Abschreiben oder Informationen weitergeben ist ohne
schriftliche Erlaubnis des Herausgebers nicht gestattet.

First edition, 1995 by: Graphic-sha Publishing Co., Ltd.
1-9-12 Kudan-kita. Chiyoda-ku, Tokyo 102 Japan

The German-English edition in 1996 by:
NIPPAN
Nippon Shuppan Hanbai Deutschland GmbH
Krefelder Straße 85
D-40549 Düsseldorf, Germany

Printed in Singapore by Toppan Printing Co., PTE Ltd.

Create Your Own Japanese Garden
Japanische Gartengestaltung

ゆばた花月亭庭園
Yubata Kagetsu-tei Inn Garden

1. Aussagekräftiges Blaustein-Arrangement im Westgarten.

2. *Ukifune* („schwimmendes Boot") *Sanzon* Arrangement im Westgarten vor den Gästezimmern.

3. Blick vom Gästezimmer in den Westgarten.

中庭　西部〈蓬壺庭〉
Inner garden west side: Hoko-tei

4. *Ryumonbaku* Wasserfall und danebenliegendes Steinarrangement im Westgarten.

Der Innengarten des *Kagetsu-tei*, einem traditionellen japanischen Hotel, ist von Gästezimmern umgeben. Um den Gästen auf jeder Seite Ungestörtheit zu garantieren, teilte der Designer diesen Teil des Gartens in zwei Hälften (Ost und West), die er unterschiedlich anlegte. Der Westgarten ist ein Teichgarten, der verschiedene Chlorit-Schist-Steinarrangements enthält. Diese stellen den *Mt. Horai* dar (einen Berg aus chinesischen Volksmärchen, auf dem uralte Wizzards leben). Der Westgarten wird *Hoko-tei* genannt (*Hoko* ist ein Synonym für *Horai*). Außerdem befinden sich hier ein *Horai* Steinarrangement, ein Grotten-Steinarrangement und ein *Ryumonbaku* Wasserfall.

Das Hauptmerkmal des Ostgartens ist ein kurvenreicher Fluß; der Garten wird *Ryusho-tei* (nach in China und Japan veranstalteten Poesie-Feiern) genannt. Die Quelle des Flusses ist ein Wasserfall. Der Fluß fließt parallel, jedoch viel ruhiger als der kraftvolle *Ryumonbaku* des Westgartens (die Wasserfälle in solch einer Paarung sind als „männlicher" und „weiblicher" Wasserfall bekannt, wobei der männliche größer ist). Direkt vor dem Wasserfall befindet sich eine Steinbrücke, um den Anschein eines Gemäldes aus indischer Tinte zu erzeugen. Der Fluß fließt in Richtung Vorderseite der Lobby und endet im Teich.

5. Steinarrangement um den Gartenteich.

1. Showy blue-stone arrangements of the western garden.
2. *Ukifune* ("floating boat") *sanzon* stone arrangement in the western garden, in front of a guest room.
3. View of the western garden from a guest room.
4. *Ryumonbaku* waterfall and nearby stone arrangements in the western garden.
5. Stone arrangements around the garden pond.

· Inner garden: Hoko-tei and Ryusho-tei
Design: Isao Yoshikawa. **Construction:** Shin'ichi Kosuge, Fujishige Ltd.; 1990.
Area: 972 square meters. **Location:** Shimoda, Shizuoka Pref.

中庭 東部〈流觴庭〉
Inner garden east side: Ryusho-tei

6. Kurviger Fluß und Steinbrücke.

7. Blaustein-Brücke.

8. Steinufer im nördlichen Teil des Gartens.

9. Der eleganter Fluß im Ostgarten.

6. Curving stream and stone bridge.
7. Blue-stone bridge.
8. Stone shore in the northern part of the garden.
9. The elegant stream of the eastern garden.
10. Western garden pond.
11. Stone arrangement forming the "female" waterfall, the source of the stream in the eastern garden.

中庭 東部〈流觴庭〉
Inner garden east side: Ryusho-tei

Wasserkörper

Die Umrandung der Teiche und fließenden Gewässer sind die wesentlichen Elemente, um die Form der Gewässer zu bestimmen.

Für wunderschöne Kurven entlang des Ufers von fließendem Gewässer ist es besser, kleine Steine zu verwenden, die die Form des Teichs hervorheben. Diese Steine sind nicht nur Uferbefestigung, sondern auch die ästhetische Abrundung des Teichs. Kürzlich wurde auch Beton als Befestigung verwendet, doch man sollte in einer Gartenlandschaft keinen Beton oder ähnliche Stoffe sichtbar verwenden. Sie werden nur ganz im Hintergrund versteckt verwendet; denn sie würden die Erscheinung des Gartens zerstören (Yoshikawa).

Water Banks

The banks of ponds and flowing water are certainly the most important elements that determine the shape of a pond.

When attempting to create beautiful curves along banks of flowing water one prefers to use smaller stones which hew to the shape of the pond. Not only do these stones protect the edge of the pond, but they must complement the pond aesthetically, as well. Recently concrete is used to form the boundaries of ponds, but in garden landscaping one never allows it, or any type of mortar, to be seen. Mortar is often used between the stones of an embankment, but it goes without saying that it is placed far back between the stones; any evidence of it on the outside would destroy the appeal of the scene. (Yoshikawa)

10. Teich im Westgarten.

11. Das Steinarrangement bildet den „weiblichen" Wasserfall, die Quelle des Flusses im Ostgarten.

The inner garden of Kagetsu-tei, a traditional Japanese inn, is enclosed by the inn's guest rooms. To ensure privacy for the guest rooms on either side, the designer divided the garden by a long artificial mountain of rocks into eastern and western sections laid out in two distinct styles. The western section is a pond garden that contains several showy chlorite-schist stone arrangements positioned to evoke images of Mount Horai, a mountain in Chinese folklore on which ageless wizards were said to reside. (The western garden is called Hoko-tei, Hoko being a synonym for Horai.) There is a Horai stone arrangement, a grotto stone arrangement, and a *ryumonbaku* waterfall.

The central feature of the eastern garden is a curving stream; the garden is called Ryusho-tei, after streamside poetry-writing banquets held in early China and Japan. The source of the stream is a waterfall, flowing parallel to but more slenderly than the more powerful *ryumonbaku* of the western garden. (The two waterfalls in such a pair are known as male and female waterfalls, the male waterfall being the larger.) Directly in front of the waterfall is a stone bridge, positioned to evoke the image of an india ink painting. The stream wends its way to the front of the lobby, emptying into the pond.

前庭
Front garden

1. *Kinkakuji* Zaun am Eingang des Grundstücks. Er paßt sehr gut zu dem Namensschild am Eingang des Gartens (links).

2. Die Steinlaterne und der Eingangsbereich vom Grundstück aus betrachtet.

Die Besitzer des *Kagetsu-tei* haben sich sehr viel Mühe gegeben, die vorbeilaufende Straße mit der Schönheit des Vorgartens zu vereinen. Die Auffahrt wurde mit großen geschnittenen Granitplatten ausgelegt und ist jetzt für Kleinbusse groß genug. Auf den hellgrünen Fliesen aus *Pyroxene Andesite* kann der Bus jetzt sogar drehen.

Obwohl der Innengarten des *Kagetsu-tei* zahlreiche Steinarrangements enthält – typisch für traditionelle Teichgärten – plante der Designer den Vorgarten sehr schlicht. Nur ein paar vertikal aufgestellte Steine zieren diesen Garten. Auf beiden Seiten des Eingangs wurde eine Steinmauer errichtet, die jeweils mit einem *Kinkakuji* Zaun bestückt wurde. Andere Merkmale im Vorgarten sind die *Yunoki* Steinlaterne im Stil der *Heian* Periode und ein *Tsukubai* Arrangement, ein im *Kamakura* Stil erbautes *Tepatsu* Steinbecken (Form einer Bettelschale). Ein sehr kreativer Aspekt im Vorgarten ist der aus weißem Sand angelegte Vollmond, der teilweise von einer Wolke aus *Kokumazasa* Bambusgras und *Dwarf Snake's Beard* (eine Form des japanischen *Snake's Beard*) abgedeckt ist.

前庭
Front garden

3. Der teilweise durch *Kokumazasa* Bambusgras abgedeckte „Vollmond".

4. *Yunoki* Steinlaterne neben dem Eingang des Hotels.

The proprietors of the Kagetsu-tei have taken great pains to blend the functionality of a driveway with the beauty of a front garden. Paved with large pieces of cut granite, the driveway is wide enough to allow a microbus to enter; the large pyroxene andesite flagstones crossing the drive permit the bus to turn.

Although the inner garden of the Kagetsu-tei contains numerous stone arrangements, as are found in a traditional pond garden, the designer gave the front garden a clean look by using few vertically positioned stones. To either side of the entrance is a stone fence topped with a Kinkakuji fence. Other features of the front garden are a Heian period-style *yunoki* stone lantern and a *tsukubai* arrangement that includes a Kamakura period-style *teppatsu* ("mendicant priest's begging bowl") stone basin. The truly creative aspect of the garden, however, is the full moon created with white sand, partially obscured by a cloud of kokumazasa bamboo grass and dwarf snake's beard (a dwarf variety of Japanese snake's beard).

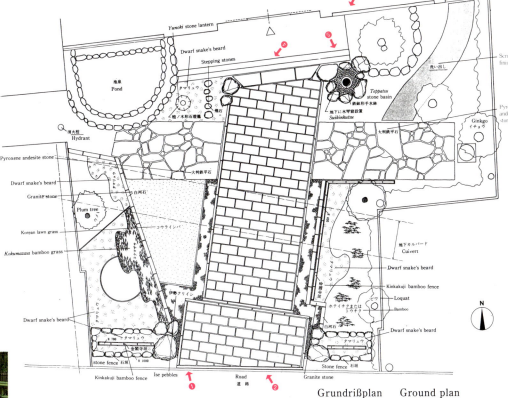

Grundrißplan   Ground plan

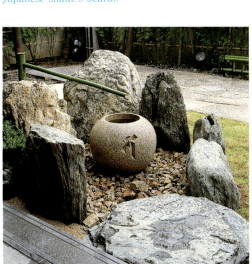

5. Steinbecken in Form einer „Bettelschale" im *Tsukubai* Arrangement neben dem Hoteleingang.

Die auf der Skizze in Rot eingezeichneten Nummern und Pfeile zeigen die Blickwinkel, aus denen die jeweiligen Aufnahmen gemacht wurden.

Numbers and signs with red on the sketch are pointing the place and direction where the photograph was taten.

1. Kinkakuji fence at the entrance to the grounds. It is well balanced with the sign bearing the inn's name, at the left.
2. Stone lantern and entrance to the grounds as viewed from the inn itself.
3. The "full moon," partially obscured by *kokumazasa* bamboo grass.
4. *Yunoki* stone lantern, near the entrance to the inn.
5. "Begging bowl" stone basin in its *tsukubai* arrangement, near the entrance to the inn.

· Front garden

Design: Isao Yoshikawa. **Construction:** Shin'ichi Kosuge, Kazuo Ebihara, Ando Stone Materials; 1990. **Area:** 315 square meters. **Location:** Shimoda, Shizuoka Pref.

濱清・瓢庵庭園
Hamasei Hisago-an Restaurant Garden

1. Das Gebiet rund um den Eingang ist mit Granitfliesen ausgelegt und mit einer *Yunoki* Steinlaterne verschönert.

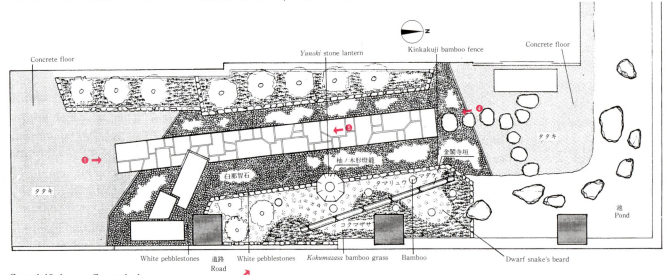

Grundrißplan   Ground plan

前庭
Front garden

2. Steinlaterne und der darunter angebrachte *Kinkakuji* Zaun.

3. Granitfliesen.

4. Eingang von der Tür zum Restaurant aus betrachtet.

1. The area around the entrance to the building grounds, enhanced by granite flagstones and a *yunoki* stone lantern.
2. Stone lantern and Kinkakuji fence below it.
3. Flagstones.
4. Entrance area, viewed from the door of the restaurant.

· Front garden
Design: Isao Yoshikawa. **Construction:** Shin'ichi Kosuge, Kazuo Ebihara, Akira Sakurai; 1991. **Area:** 87.5 square meters.
Location: Taito-ku, Tokyo.

Die Besitzer dieses im japanischen Stil eingerichteten Restaurants wollten den Garten an die traditionelle Atmosphäre des Restaurants angepaßt haben. Das Restaurant befindet sich im ersten Stock eines Bürogebäudes in der Stadt. Der Designer wollte die Gäste vergessen lassen, daß sie sich eigentlich in einem Bürogebäude befinden. Obwohl der schon vorhandene Teich verblieb, ist das Hauptmerkmal des Gartens der Fußweg, der sehr schlicht mit Fliesen und hartem schwarzem Schiefer ausgelegt ist. Entlang dem Gebäude laufen zwei mit Pflanzen eingefaßte Steinwege (diese Pflanzen müssen regelmäßig erneuert werden, da die Pflanzen aufgrund des Lichtmangels schnell absterben). Andere Elemente im Garten sind z.B. die *Yunoki* Steinlaterne, der *Kinkakuji-* und ein Bambuszweigzaun sowie verschiedene Bambuspflanzen. Die Zweige des Bambus wurden nicht geschnitten, da der Baum in regelmäßigen Abständen erneuert wird.

The owners of this Japanese-style restaurant, located on the first floor of an urban building, wanted the garden revamped in a manner appropriate to the traditional atmosphere of the establishment. In line with this, the designer's intention was to help visitors forget that they are actually in an office building. Although the original pond remains, the primary feature of the redesigned garden is the pathways, laid out very formally with flagstones of hard black slate. Along the building itself are two levels of tuff stone pavements lined with plants (that have to be transplanted regularly due to the lack of sunlight). Other features in the garden include a *yunoki* stone lantern, Kinkakuji and bamboo branch fences, and a display of stout bamboo plants. The branches of the bamboo are left uncut, and the entire plants are replaced with new ones on a regular schedule.

帰心亭庭園
Kishin-tei garden

1. Gartenzaun, Steinbecken und Bambusboden.

Im fünften Stock des o. g. Gebäudes ist der schmale *Kishin-tei* Garten auf einem Balkon angelegt. Der Designer mußte beim Layout mehrere Punkte in Betracht ziehen – einige davon hat er sich selbst vorgegeben: Das Material mußte wegen des Standorts des Gartens leicht sein; dazu sollte es eine Kombination aus traditionellen sowie modernen Elementen sein, um den Garten nicht zu typisch für japanische Restaurants werden zu lassen. Außerdem soll der Garten seine Gäste (wie auch der Vorgarten des Restaurants) vergessen lassen, daß sie sich in einem Bürogebäude in der Stadt befinden. Der Designer löste das Gewichtsproblem, indem er eine Auswahl von leichten Quarz-Trachyt-Steinen verwendete. Der letztgenannte Punkt wurde durch einen „Fischnetz"-Bambuszaun bestens gelöst. Dieser Zaun ist ein traditionelles Muster in Japan und den Zäunen nachgebaut, die an den Küsten stehen, um die Fischernetze zu trocknen. Das Restaurant befindet sich in der Nähe des *Senso-ji* Tempels in *Asakusa*, in dem der *Bodhisattva Kannon* angebetet wurde. Am neben der Stadt fließenden *Sumida* Fluß steht auch eine *Kannon* Statue, auf die die Fischer ihre Netze zum Trocknen ausgebreitet haben. Somit besteht also ein unmittelbarer Bezug des Zauns zur Umgebung. Die diagonal angeordneten Stützpfeiler sind die markanten Punkte des Designs. In der Mitte des Gartens, zwischen dem Zaun und dem Bambusboden, befindet sich ein Steinarrangement mit einem *Teppatsu* Steinbecken, das aus einer ehemaligen Fünf-Stein *Stupa* der *Heian* Periode stammt. Daneben ist unter der Erde ein *Suikinkutsu* (ein kleiner unterirdischer Raum in den das Wasser tropft), und dadurch Echogeräusche erzielt werden.

2. Arrangement mit *Teppatsu* Steinbecken. Die Pflanzen sind *Kokumazasa* Bambusgräser.

1. Garden fence, stone basin, and bamboo flooring.
2. *Teppatsu* stone basin in its arrangement. The plants are *kokumazasa* bamboo grass.
3. The "fish net" bamboo fence.
4. Plum tree and bamboo fence, viewed from inside the restaurant.

帰心亭庭園
Kishin-tei garden

Located on the fifth floor of the building mentioned on the previous pages, the Kishin-tei restaurant has a small garden on its balcony. The designer had several conditions to meet in laying out this garden, some of them of his own making: the garden materials had to be lightweight, given the location; a combination of the traditional with the modern would be preferable, to avoid a layout overly typical of Japanese restaurants; and, as with the front garden of the same building, the garden should enable guests to forget that they are in an urban building.

The designer solved the weight problem by using a light variety of quartz trachyte for the garden stones. The solution to the last-mentioned condition was in the design of the background. A "fish net" bamboo fence, a traditional Japanese design imitative of fishers' nets drying on the seashore, was used. The restaurant also happens to be near Senso-ji Temple, in Asakusa, where the bodhisattva Kannon is worshiped, and along the nearby Sumida River there is a Kannon statue where fishermen hung their nets to dry; the fence thus has numerous local associations. The diagonally arranged support poles lend an air of boldness to the design.

In the center of the garden, between the fence and a square of bamboo flooring, is a stone arrangement containing a *teppatsu* stone basin of the author's design, "recycled" from part of a Heian-period five-stone stupa. Near this, underground, is a *suikinkutsu*, a small underground chamber in which water droplets are allowed to fall and echo.

3. Der „Fischnetz"-Bambuszaun.

4. Pflaumenbaum und Bambuszaun aus dem Restaurant heraus betrachtet.

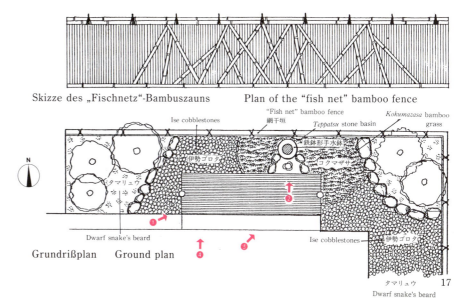
Skizze des „Fischnetz"-Bambuszauns   Plan of the "fish net" bamboo fence

Grundrißplan   Ground plan

- Kishin-tei restaurant garden
Design: Isao Yoshikawa. **Construction:** Shin'ichi Kosuge, Kazuo Ebihara, Akira Sakurai; 1991. **Area:** 18 square meters. **Location:** Taito-ku, Tokyo.

大蓮寺庭園
Dairen-ji Temple Garden

1. Blick von oben auf die zwei den trockenen Teich überquerenden Wege.

2. Der gefliste Weg vom Haupttor aus betrachtet mit einer Schwarz-Pinie im Hintergrund.

Der Vorgarten des ehrbaren *Dairen-ji* Tempels ist im Stil der Lehre der „Pure Land" Sekte angelegt. Der mit Fliesen ausgelegte Weg zum Tempel teilt sich in zwei Richtungen auf – einer führt zu den Wohnräumen des Priesters, der andere zur Empfangshalle des Tempels. Um dieser Fläche eine attraktive Erscheinung zu verleihen, führte der Designer die beiden Wege über einen trockenen Teich, der die Form einer „glücklichen Wolke" hat. Der Weg geht über dem Teich in eine Brücke aus geschnittenem Stein über. Die Brücke zu den Wohnräumen läuft genau vor dem Schildkröteninsel-Steinarrangement (ein weiterer Bestandteil des „Glückssymbols") über den Teich. Die im *Dairen-ji* Garten verwendeten Steine wurden alle vom Oberpriester des Tempels zusammengetragen. Sieben oder acht davon sind rote Steine, die der Designer für die Schildkröteninsel verwendete. Vor dem Lehrzimmer wurde eine viereckige Granitplatte ausgelegt. Wiederum davor steht das *Rendai* Steinbecken in einem *Tsukubai* Arrangement. Die *Oribe* Steinlaterne ist im Stil des frühen 17. Jahrhunderts gefertigt.

The front garden of Dairen-ji is laid out in a style appropriate to the Pure Land sect doctrine of this venerable temple. The flagstone-paved approach to the temple divides into two paths, one leading to the priest's living quarters, the other to a reception room. To give this area an attractive appearance, the designer had the two paths traverse a dry pond, which is laid out in the form of an "auspicious cloud." The flagstone paths become cut-stone bridges as they cross the pond, the bridge to the priest's quarters a Chinese-style one that passes in front of a turtle island stone arrangement, another element of auspicious symbolism.

The stones used in the stone arrangements in the Dairen-ji garden were all gathered by the head priest of the temple. Seven or eight of these are red stones, which the designer used for the turtle island. A small square of granite has been laid in front of

前庭〈二十五菩薩来迎之庭〉
Front garden: Garden of th Descent of the Twenty-Five Bodhisattvas

3. Arrangement des trockenen Wasserfalls mit *Amida Sanzon* Motiv.

4. *Rendai* Steinbecken im *Tsukubai* Arrangement.

5. Die große Brücke aus geschnittenen Steinen aus dem trockenen Teich heraus betrachtet.

6. Schildkröteninsel-Steinarrangement aus roten Steinen.

the entrance to the study, and in front of this are a *rendai* stone basin in a *tsukubai* arrangement and an *oribe* stone lantern in the style of the early seventeenth century. The south side of the garden has a beautiful, large black pine, under which the designer placed a dry-waterfall stone arrangement, including a *sanzon* motif, with Amida (the primary buddha of the Pure Land sect) in the center.

1. View from above of the two paths crossing the dry pond.
2. Flagstone-paved approach from the main gate, with a black pine in the background.
3. Dry waterfall arrangement with Amida *sanzon* motif.
4. *Rendai* stone basin in its *tsukubai* arrangement.
5. Main cut-stone bridge viewed from the dry pond.
6. Turtle island stone arrangement, using red stones.

• Front garden: Garden of the Descent of the Twenty-Five Bodhisattvas
Design: Isao Yoshikawa. **Construction:** Shin'ichi Kosuge, Kazuo Ebihara, Akira Sakurai; 1991. **Area:** 330 square meters. **Location:** Urayasu, Chiba Pref.

中庭〈二河白道之庭〉
Inner garden: Two-River White-Path Garden

1. Der Innengarten mit dem „Pure Land" Arrangement auf der gegenüberliegenden Seite.
2. Der „weiße Steg".
3. Die beiden Flüsse mit dem darüberlaufenden Steg.

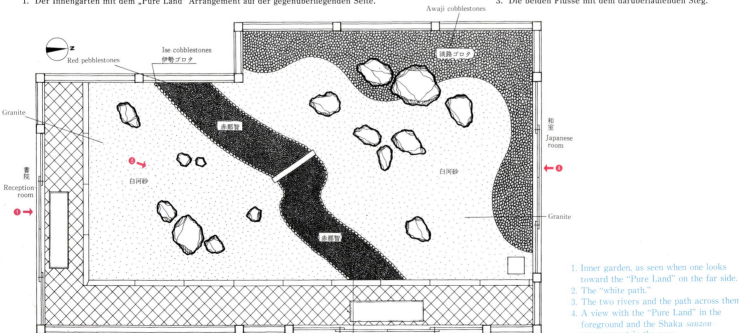

Grundrißplan Ground plan

1. Inner garden, as seen when one looks toward the "Pure Land" on the far side.
2. The "white path."
3. The two rivers and the path across them.
4. A view with the "Pure Land" in the foreground and the Shaka *sanzon* arrangement in the rear.
5. Amida *sanzon* arrangement.

中庭〈二河白道之庭〉
Inner garden: Two-River White-Path Garden

Von den Tempelgebäuden umgeben, kann der *Dairenji's* Innengarten, der keine Vorder- bzw. Rückseite besitzt, von drei Seiten betrachtet werden. Der Designer will die unterschiedlichen Lehren des Buddhismus darstellen. Das eine Motiv spiegelt die Lehre vom „Garten mit zwei Flüssen und weißem Steg" wider, die besagt, daß es einen Fluß aus Feuer und einen Fluß aus einer gefährlichen Flüssigkeit gibt, die diese Welt vom „Pure Land" (Paradies) abgrenzen. Obwohl kein Mensch ohne Hilfe *Amidas* diese Flüsse überqueren kann, erscheint durch Singen bestimmter Psalmen ein weißer Steg, der in das „Pure Land" führt. In diesem Garten repräsentiert die der Empfangshalle zugewandte Seite unsere Welt. Ein *Shaka Sanzon* Arrangement (eine Buddha-Statue) steht in diesem Garten. Die andere Seite repräsentiert das „Pure Land" mit einem *Amida Sanzon* Arrangement. Die beiden Flüsse aus roten und blauen Steinen trennen die beiden Welten, vereinen sie jedoch gleichzeitig durch den weißen Granitsteg.

Selbst wenn ein Betrachter nicht mit dieser Lehre vertraut ist und die religiöse Bedeutung nicht erfaßt, so ist der Gesamteindruck des Gartens wunderschön.

Surrounded by temple buildings, Dairenji's inner garden may be appreciated from three sides and thus does not have a real front or back. The designer attempted to express the doctrines of the various sects of Buddhism in the garden's layout. One motif reflects the "two-river white-path" doctrine of the Pure Land sect, which teaches that there is a river of fire and one with a violent current that separate this world from the Pure Land, or paradise. Although human beings cannot cross the rivers without the aid of Amida, they can chant a set prayer, and a white path will appear, leading to the Pure Land. In this garden, the side near the reception room represents the present world and contains a Shaka (the historical Buddha) *sanzon* arrangement, and the side opposite this is the Pure Land, with an Amida *sanzon* arrangement. Two "rivers" of red and blue stones separate the two worlds, but joining them is a white path of granite.

Even if a visitor is not familiar with this doctrine and thus cannot interpret the religious significance of the dry-landscape arrangement, the overall effect is one of great beauty.

· Inner garden: Two-River White-Path Garden
Design: Isao Yoshikawa. **Construction:** Ishiroku; 1977. **Area:** 42.6 square meters. **Location:** Urayasu, Chiba Pref.

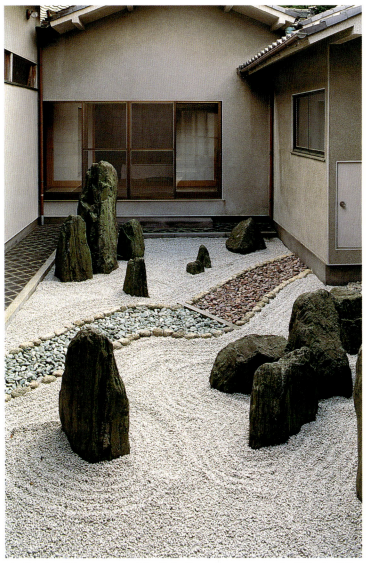

4. „Pure Land" Arrangement und das *Shaka Sanzon* Arrangement weiter hinten im Bild.

5. *Amida Sanzon* Arrangement.

青松院庭園
Seisho-in Temple Garden

1. Die Uferbefestigung aus Stein trägt hier zur Schönheit des Gartens bei.

1. The embankment stone arrangements shown here add to the beauty of the garden.
2. Waterfall arrangement in the eastern section of the garden.

Der *Seisho-in* Tempel (*Soto Zen* Buddhismus), wurde Ende der *Muromachi* Periode erbaut. Gemäß den Wünschen des derzeitigen Oberpriesters (*Taido Yasushi*, ein Direktor des Japanischen Gartenforschungsinstituts) wurde der Nordgarten der Tempel-Zuflucht (*Shogai-tei* genannt) mit einem kurvigen Teich angelegt (einem Merkmal der *Muromachi* Periode). Der Teich wird von einer natürlichen Quelle gespeist. Der Garten besitzt zahlreiche Steinarrangements, die alle aus heimischem *Andesite* erbaut sind. Mit Ausnahme des großen Steins des Wasserfallarrangements im westlichen Garten sind die Steine relativ klein. Der Designer wollte mit dieser Formation die schlichte Eleganz einer chinesischen Tintenzeichnung ausdrücken. Ein spiralförmiges Arrangement (ein Leitmotiv der *Muromachi* Periode), steht auf einem Hügel im vorderen Teil des Gartens. Eine Brücke aus blauem Stein liegt über dem Mittelteil des Teichs neben dem Kranich-Schildkröteninsel-Arrangement. Das Schildkröteninsel-Arrangement steht direkt vor dem Wasserfallarrangement im Westen. Der kleinere Stein, der den Kopf des Kranichs darstellt, schafft eine Distanz zum zweiten Wasserfallarrangement, welches direkt dahinter plaziert ist.

A temple of the Soto Zen Buddhism, Seisho-in was built at the end of the Muromachi period. Based on the wishes of the current head priest of the temple (Taido Yasushi, a director of the Japanese Garden Research Society), the northern garden of the temple sanctuary, known as the Shogai-tei, was laid out with a curved pond, a feature of Muromachi-period gardens. The pond is fed by a natural spring. The garden has numerous stone arrangements, all of locally quarried andesite, and, except for the large stone of the waterfall arrangement in the western part of the garden, the stones are all relatively small. The designer's intention was that these arrangements evoke the elegant simplicity of a Chinese ink painting.

The designer placed a spiral stone arrangement, a motif in vogue during the Muromachi period, atop a built-up rock hill in the front of the garden. A bridge of blue stone spans the middle portion of the garden pond, where a crane-turtle island stone arrangement is also found. A turtle island stone arrangement has been set in front of the western waterfall arrangement, and two stones forming a crane arrangement are found in the eastern section of the pond. The smaller stone representing the head of the crane helps create a sense of distance for a second waterfall arrangement placed behind it.

本堂北庭〈松嶽庭〉
Northern garden of the temple sanctuary: Shogaku-tei

2. Wasserfallarrangement im westlichen Teil des Gartens.

3. Brücke aus blauen Steinen mit spiralförmigem Steinarrangement im Hintergrund.

3. Bridge of blue stone, with spiral stone arrangement in the background.
4. Crane stone arrangement.
5. Traditional turtle island stone arrangement in the middle section of the pond.
6. Waterfall arrangement in the western section of the garden.

- Northern garden of the temple sanctuary: Shogaku-tei
Design: Isao Yoshikawa. **Construction:** Shuji Matsui, Yasushi Fukushima; 1979.
Area: 648 square meters. **Location:** Kofu, Yamanshi Pref.

4. Kranich-Steinarrangement.

5. Traditionelles Schildkröteninsel-Steinarrangement in der Mitte des Teichs.

6. Wasserfallarrangement im westlichen Teil des Gartens.

書院北庭〈青龍庭〉
Northern garden of the reception room: Seiryu-tei

1. Gesamtansicht des eindrucksvollen Steinarrangements mit Azaleen.

2. Teich und Uferbefestigung.

1. An overall view of the showy stone arrangements and azaleas of the garden.
2. Pond and embankment stones.
3. *Ryumonbaku* waterfall arrangement, the main feature of the garden.
4. Built-up rock hill and embankment stone arrangement.
5. Grotto stone arrangement in an embankment.
6. Waterfall stone arrangement viewed from the pondside.

・ Northern garden of the reception room: Seiryu-tei
Design: Isao Yoshikawa. **Construction:** Shuji Matsui, Reiichi Kagami; 1978. **Area:** 260 square meters. **Location:** Kofu, Yamanshi Pref.

書院北庭〈青龍庭〉
Northern garden of the reception room: Seiryu-tei

3. *Ryumonbaku* Wasserfallarrangement, das Hauptmerkmal des Gartens.

5. Grotten-Steinarrangement in der Uferbefestigung.

4. Aufgestellter Felsenhügel mit Uferbefestigung.

6. Wasserfallarrangement aus dem trockenen Teich heraus betrachtet.

Der Nordgarten der Empfangshalle ist auf einem steilen Hang angelegt. Unter Verwendung des steilen Anstiegs schaffte der Designer ein ausdrucksstarkes Layout, das charakteristisch für die *Momoyama* Periode ist. Das dem Zen-Geist entsprechende *Ryumonbaku* Wasserfallarrangement ist das Hauptelement des Gartens. Im Einklang mit chinesischen Legenden enthält der *Ryumonbaku*, das Wasserfallarrangement, in diesem Garten drei verschiedene Ebenen (*Ryumon* ist ein Abschnitt des „Gelben Flusses", der viele Stromschnellen enthält; *baku* bedeutet Stromschnelle oder Kaskade). Wasserfälle (auch trockene Formationen wie hier zu sehen) bestehen aus Hauptsteinen, die das Wasser spenden. Diese drei Steine in dieser Formation sind so plaziert, um Entfernung zu schaffen. Das große Arrangement beinhaltet auch einen Stein mit der Form eines Karpfens, der direkt am Grund der Wasserfälle steht. Die Uferbefestigungssteine wurden so angelegt, daß sie Drei-Dimensionalität erzeugen. Außerdem sind einige Steine diagonal ausgerichtet, um Bewegung in die Formation zu bringen, wenn man sie aus verschiedenen Blickwinkeln betrachtet. Auch Grottenarrangements sind hier und rund um den Tempel unauffällig in die Formationen mit eingebaut. Großflächig gepflanzte, geschnittene Azaleen verdecken den Hügel.

The northern garden of the temple's reception room is spread out over a steep slope. Exploiting the high ground, the designer laid out the garden in a showy style characteristic of the Momoyama period. A *ryumonbaku* waterfall arrangement, appropriate to the Zen spirit, is the main feature of the garden. Consistent with the Chinese legends concerning *ryumonbaku* (*Ryumon* is a section of the Yellow River containing rapids; *baku* means "rapids" or "cascade"), the arrangement in this garden contains three levels of waterfalls. Waterfall stone arrangements (including dry arrangements, as here), include a stone from the top of which the water falls (or would fall). The three such stones in the arrangement here are each positioned to give the impression of distinct water flows. The overall arrangement also contains a carp stone—a stone representative of a carp attempting to ascend the falls—at the bottom.

The designer positioned the embankment stones to the left of the waterfalls to emphasize the sense of perspective in the garden, the diagonally placed stones giving the embankment a sense of movement when viewed from certain angles. Some of the embankments include grotto stone arrangements, common in the region around the temple, although they have been deliberately designed not to be conspicuous. Azalea plants trimmed to one large shape set off the built-up rocks.

庫裡南庭〈酬恩之庭〉
Southern garden of the priest's living quarters: Shuon no Niwa

1. Steinarrangement und Steinbecken.

Der Garten südlich der Priester-Wohnräume wurde rund um eine japanische Rot-Pinie angelegt, die der Priester von seinem Vater anläßlich seiner Anstellung in diesem Tempel geschenkt bekam. Ein münzenförmiges Steinbecken, das der Designer 1976 selbst entworfen und dem Tempel geschenkt hat, ist ebenfalls in das Steinarrangement mit eingebaut. (Auf Seite 61 finden Sie unter *Isao Yoshikawa's Chozubachi* Steinbecken, durch *Graphic-sha* veröffentlicht, eine genaue Beschreibung dieses Steinbeckens.) Es wurde auf einen flachen Stein in der Mitte des Gartens aufgestellt und mit Steinen umgeben. Die Rot-Pinie bleibt durch das Arrangement sichtbar.

Eine würfelförmige Steinlaterne, die dem Tempel zu Beginn der Edo-Periode geschenkt wurde, ist im hinteren Teil des Gartens vor dem Grab des seinerzeit verpflichteten Priesters aufgestellt.

The garden to the south of the priest's living quarters was designed around a Japanese red pine given to the head priest by his father on the occasion of his installation at the temple and a coin-shaped stone basin made by the designer in 1976 and presented to the temple (see page 61 of Isao Yoshikawa's *Chozubachi/Stone Basins*, published by Graphic-sha, for a complete description of this basin and the characters on it). The basin was placed on a flat stone in the center of the garden and stones were arranged around it, with the red pine visible between them.

A square house-shaped stone lantern, presented to the temple at the beginning of the Edo period, sits toward the rear of the garden in front of the grave of the priest of the temple at the time.

1. Stone arrangement and stone basin.
2. Stone arrangement and lantern.
3. Full view of the garden.
4. Stone basin with four characters carved on its surface.

- Southern garden of the priest's living quarters: Shuon no Tei
Design: Isao Yoshikawa. **Construction:** Ichiro Takahashi, Goichi Iketani, Watanabe Construction; 1977. **Area:** 162 square meters. **Location:** Kofu, Yamanshi Pref.

2. Steinarrangement und Laterne.

3. Gesamtansicht des Gartens.

4. Steinbecken mit vier in die Abdeckung eingravierten Symbolen.

東漸寺庭園
Tozen-ji Temple Garden

本堂南庭〈十二神将之庭〉
Southern garden of the temple sanctuary:
Garden of Twelve Generals

1. Diese wunderschöne Trockenlandschaft ist typisch für einen Zen-Tempel.

3. Abstraktes Schildkröteninsel-Steinarrangement unter der japanischen Schwarz-Pinie.

Tozen-ji ist ein Tempel der *Rinzai* Sekte (im Tantrischen Buddhismus gegründet), die dem Zen-Buddhismus angehört. Die Gestaltung der Haupthalle (*Buddha Yakushi Nyorai*) zeigt die auch. Diese Art ist typisch für Zen-Tempel. Im Garten sind 12 Stein-Arrangements, welche die „12 Generäle" symbolisieren, die wiederum *Yakushi Nyorai* beschützen. Ein fächerförmiges Arrangement liegt vor der *Yakushi Nyorai* Statue.

Eine schon vorhandene alte japanische Schwarz-Pinie ersetzt die Blumen in diesem Garten (angelehnt an die Blumen, die ein Grab oder einen buddhistischen Altar schmücken). Ein Insel-Steinarrangement, das auch als abstraktes Schildkröteninsel-Steinarrangement betrachtet werden kann, wurde neben dem Baum aufgestellt.

2. Ein Arrangement aus sechs Steinen mit sandsteinförmigen Elementen.

Tozen-ji is a temple of the Rinzai sect of Zen Buddhism. It was at one time, however, associated with Tantric Buddhism, and the principal image in the main hall of temple is still the buddha Yakushi Nyorai. The garden is laid out on a rectangular piece of land to the south of the main hall, in the dry-landscape style typical of Zen temples. In the garden are twelve stone arrangements representing the "Twelve Generals" who protect Yakushi Nyorai. The arrangements are spread out in a fan shape with a point in front of the Yakushi Nyorai statue as the central pivot.

An old Japanese black pine, on the grounds before this garden was created, remains as a "flower offering" (analogous to flowers placed on a grave or Buddhist altar) to Yakushi Nyorai. An island stone arrangement, which can also be seen as an abstract turtle island stone arrangement, has been placed near this tree.

1. This beautiful dry-landscape arrangement is characteristic of Zen temples.
2. Sandbar-shaped rock area and six-stone arrangement.
3. Abstract turtle island stone arrangement centered on a Japanese black pine.

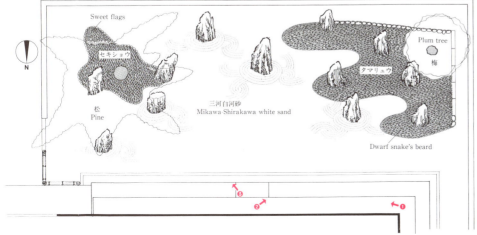

Grundrißplan   Ground plan

· Southern garden of the temple sanctuary: Garden of the Twelve Generals
Design: Isao Yoshikawa. **Construction:** Nakajima Landscaping; 1988. **Area:** 230 square meters. **Location:** Kitakoma-gun, Yamanashi Pref.

心経堂前庭〈補陀落庭〉
Front garden of Shingyo Hall: Fudaraku-tei garden

1. Fünf der sechs Steine des Arrangements im südlichen Teil des Gartens.

Die *Shingyo* („Herz-Sutra") Halle steht im Osten des Tempelgrundstücks und ist nach Westen ausgerichtet. Der Hallen-Vorgarten ist als trockene Landschaft mit einem Trockenteich aus kleinen Steinen angelegt. Die Bodenbepflanzung ist durch große Steine in gekurvten Linien vom Teich abgegrenzt (der Teich hat die Form eines Drachens). Wie das beiliegende Diagramm zeigt, führt ein Weg über den Teich zum Eingang der Halle und teilt den Garten dabei in eine Süd- und eine Nordhälfte, die jeweils unterschiedlich angelegt sind.

Der Garten soll den *Mount Fudaraku* (Skt. *potalaka*) darstellen, ein dem *Kannon* im Ozean südlich von Indien geweihter Fels. Der südliche Teil neben dem Weg wird "*The garden of the six kannons*" genannt. Die Steine sind zu jeweils drei Steinen im Trockenteich, einem Stein auf der Insel und zu zwei Steinen auf der Halbinsel verteilt.

Der Nordgarten wird "*The seven-five-three garden*" gemäß der Anzahl an Steinen in den drei Arrangements genannt. Je größer der Abstand zum Gebäude wird, desto größer werden die Steine. Dadurch erzielt man Drei-Dimensionalität. Das Sieben-Stein-Arrangement beinhaltet ein stehendes Steinbecken. Da dieses Becken nur aus ganz bestimmten Blickwinkeln zu sehen ist, weckt diese Formation zusätzlich Interesse. Das zylindrische Becken hat den *Sanskrit* Brief *sa* eingeritzt, den Brief der *Bodhisattva* Kannon. Die *Oribe* Steinlaterne und die *Kinkakuji*- und *Kenninji* Zäune sind weitere Merkmale in diesem Garten.

2. Gesamtansicht des Gartens.

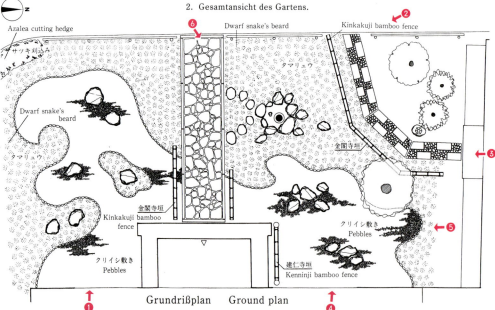

Grundrißplan Ground plan

心経堂前庭〈補陀落庭〉
Front garden of Shingyo Hall: Fudaraku-tei garden

3. Gesamtansicht des Gartens mit *Kinkakuji* Zaun und dem Steinweg, der zu den Wohnräumen des Priesters führt.

4. Fünf-Stein-Arrangement (im Vordergrund) und das Sieben-Stein-Arrangement im nördlichen Teil des Gartens.

5. Drei-, Fünf- und Sieben-Stein-Arrangement und *Kenninji* Zaun (links).

6. Blick auf das Sieben-Stein-Arrangement mit dem stehenden Steinbecken.

    Shingyo ("heart sutra") Hall stands on the eastern side of the temple grounds, facing west. The hall's front garden employs the dry-landscape style, with a dry pond of small stones separated from an area of ground cover by curved line (a "dragon pattern curve") of larger stones. As the accompanying diagram indicates, a flagstone path leading to the hall's entrance cuts across the curve, dividing the garden into north and south sections, each of which is laid out with a distinct theme.
    The garden is intended to represent Mount Fudaraku (Skt., *potalaka*), a mythical site sacred to Kannon in the ocean south of India. The southern side of the flagstone path is called the Garden of the Six Kannons, who are signified by six stones in a spread-out arrangement (three stones in the pebbled area, one on the "island," and two on the "peninsula"). The northern side of the path is called the Seven-Five-Three Garden, after the respective numbers of stones in the three arrangements in this section. The greater the distance from the building, the larger the stones, which results in a sense of perspective. The seven-stone arrangement includes a standing stone basin; the fact that the basin can be seen only from certain directions makes the arrangement that much more interesting. The cylindrical basin has carved in it (by the garden's designer) the Sanskrit letter *sa*, which is the letter of the bodhisattva Kannon.
    Other features of the garden include an old-style *oribe* stone lantern and Kinkakuji and Kenninji fences.

1. Five of the six stones of the arrangement in the southern section of the garden.
2. Overall view of the garden.
3. Overall view of the garden, with Kinkakuji fence and stone path leading to the priest's quarters.
4. Five-stone arrangement (*foreground*) and seven-stone arrangement in the northern section of the garden.
5. Three-, five-, and seven-stone arrangements and Kenninji fence (*left*).
6. View of the seven-stone arrangement with the standing stone basin visible.

• Front garden of Shingyo Hall: Fudaraku-tei garden
Fudaraku-tei garden
Design: Isao Yoshikawa. **Construction:** Nakajima Landscaping; 1988. **Area:** 200 square meters. **Location:** Kitakoma-gun, Yamanashi Pref.

光明寺庭園
Komyo-ji Temple Garden

1. Gesamtansicht des Gartens mit seinen acht Steinen, die die Erscheinung des Buddhas *Amida* widerspiegeln.

Während der *Kamakura* Periode vom Buddhistenpriester *Kishu Ryochu* erbaut, ist der *Komyo-ji* Tempel das Hauptquartier der „Pure Land" Sekte. Die nach Westen ausgerichtete Haupthalle wurde um ca. 1700 gebaut und ist das größte alte Gebäude in Kamakura. Der Südgarten der Haupthalle wird hier beschrieben.

Anläßlich des zehnten Geburtstags des Japanischen Gartenforschungsinstituts wurde dieser Garten aufgebaut. Der Designer wählte eine Trockenlandschaft mit blauen Kristall-Schist-Steinen, die vom Oberhaupt gespendet wurden. Es sollte ein Steinarrangement, angelehnt an ein Kunstmotiv des „Pure Land" Buddhismus, nachgebaut werden (Thema: „*Mida* überquert die Berge"). Das ist eines der vielen Gemälde, die den Buddha *Amida* nachstellen, der kommt, um die Welt zu retten. Dieses Steinarrangement zeigt, wie der Buddha, begleitet von den *Bodhisattvas Kannon* und *Seishi*, majestätisch über den Berg schreitet. Glücklicherweise ist einer der blauen Steine groß genug, um *Amida* zu repräsentieren.

Zwei Steine stehen für weitere *Bodhisattvas*, und die verbleibenden fünf Steine stellen Berge dar. Vier der fünf Berge, die auch fünf frühere Priester der „Pure Land" Sekte symbolisieren, stehen im weißen Sand. Die gepflanzten japanischen Schwarz-Pinien ersetzen die Blumen (analog zu den Blumen auf buddhistischen Altären und Gräbern).

Da die Haupthalle des Tempels etwas erhaben gebaut ist, wurde die Oberfläche des Sands als zusätzlicher Blickfang mit verschiedenen Mustern verschönert. Direkt vor dem Eingang befindet sich ein über 30 Meter langer Weg aus sandsteinfarbenen Fliesen, der die lilafarbenen Wolken am Himmel bei *Amidas* Ankunft symbolisiert. Die Fliesen sind aus Diorit, der Mörtel ist rot-ockerfarben. Außerdem wurde eine Azaleen-Hecke gepflanzt.

1. Overall view of the garden with its eight stones representing the advent of the buddha Amida.
2. "Mountains" set in white sand.

2. „Berge", in weißen Sand gesetzt.

〈来迎五祖の庭〉
Raigo Goso no Niwa

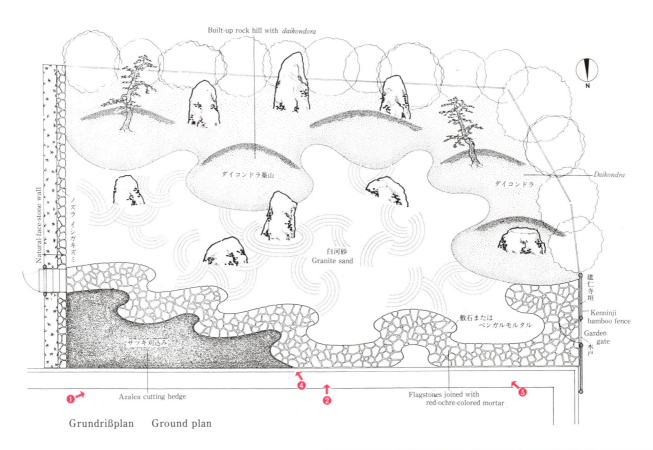

Grundrißplan Ground plan

Founded during the Kamakura period by Buddhist priest Kishu Ryochu, Komyo-ji temple is the headquarters of the Pure Land sect. The main hall, which faces west, was built in about 1700 and is the largest old building in Kamakura. The south garden of the main hall is described here.

The garden was designed in conjunction with the celebration of the tenth anniversary of the founding of the Japanese Garden Research Society. The designer had the garden laid out in the dry-landscape style, using blue crystalline schist stones donated by a parishioner to create a stone arrangement patterned after an artistic motif unique to Pure Land Buddhism: "Mida Crossing the Mountains." This is one of a number of types of paintings depicting the buddha Amida coming to save the world; in this motif Amida is shown coming across the mountains in great majesty, accompanied by the bodhisattvas Kannon and Seishi. Fortunately, one of the donated blue stones was large enough to represent Amida. Two others were used for the bodhisattvas, and five more for five mountains. Four of the five "mountains," which also represent five early priests of the Pure Land sect, are set in white sand. Japanese black pines were planted nearby as "flower offerings" (analogous to flowers placed on a grave or Buddhist altar).

Since the main hall of the temple is built well above ground level, the designer laid out the surface of the garden to provide a visually interesting view from above. Directly in front of the hall is a sandbar-shaped flagstone area some thirty meters long representing the purple clouds in the sky on the occasion of Amida's advent. The flagstones are diorite, and the mortar of the joints between them is colored with red ocher. The garden also includes an azalea hedge.

3. The large stone in the center of the background represents Amida, with the bodhisattvas Kannon (on the right) and Seishi (on the left).
4. The slanted stone on the left is, in stone arrangement terminology, a unifying stone; it pulls together the arrangement.

· Raigo Goso no Niwa
Design: Isao Yoshikawa. **Construction:** Shuji Matsui, members of the Japanese Garden Research Society; 1973. **Area:** 300 square meters. **Location:** Kamakura, Kanagawa Pref.

3. Der große Stein repräsentiert *Amida*, begleitet von den Bodhisattvas *Kannon* (rechts) und *Seishi* (links).

4. Der kleine Stein links im Bild ist (in Fachsprache ausgedrückt) ein Zusatzstein, der das Arrangement zusammen hält.

鶴岡八幡宮庭園
Tsurugaoka Hachiman-gu Shrine Garden

1. Gesamtansicht des Gartens.

2. Bootsförmiger Stein, und der Bambuszweigzaun stellt das Meer dar.

Zum dreißigsten Geburtstag des Japanischen Gartenforschungsinstituts wurde dieser kleine Vorgarten fertiggestellt. Sorgfältig ausgesuchte Materialien sollen eine elegante würdige Atmosphäre für den *Tsuruoka Hachiman-gu* Schrein bilden. Der Designer verwendete für den Weg durch den Garten vom Tor aus bis zum Eingang der Empfangshalle Granitfliesen für ein angenehmes leichtes Laufen. Links neben dem Eingang (von außen betrachtet) befindet sich ein *Tsukubai* Arrangement mit einem *Kesa* Steinbecken im Stil der *Kamakura* Periode. Der Stein vor dem Becken ist V-förmig.

Ein weiteres Merkmal im Garten ist der sich rechts neben dem Eingang befindliche bootsförmige Stein. Dieser große Stein wird von einem niedrigen Bambuszweigzaun – der das Meer, auf dem das Boot schwimmt – darstellt. Ein Teil des Gartens ist von einem im *Kyoto* Stil gefertigten *Kenninji* Zaun eingefaßt, der mit einem *Cryptomeria* Sichtschutzzaun besetzt ist.

1. Overall view of the garden.
2. Boat-shaped stone and bamboo branch fence representing the sea.
3. The Kenninji fence provides visual beauty as well as privacy.
4. *Teppo* fence whose individual poles are in the shape of tea whisks.
5. *Kesa* stone basin in its *tsukubai* arrangement.

書院前庭〈磐舟之庭〉
Front garden of the reception room:
Stone Boat Garden

3. Der *Kenninji* Zaun ist nicht nur schön, sondern dient auch als Sichtschutz.

4. *Teppo*, Zaun in Form eines Tee-Besens.

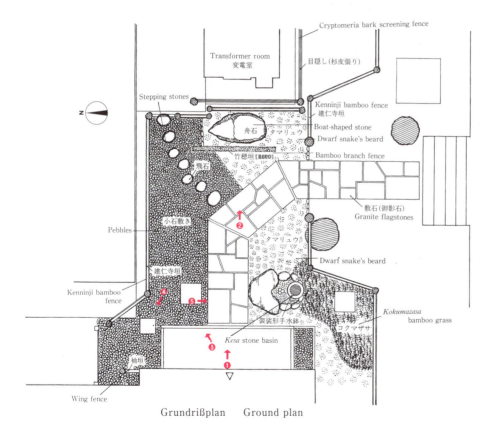

Grundrißplan   Ground plan

5. *Kesa* Steinbecken in einem *Tsukubai* Arrangement.

Completed on the occasion of the thirtieth anniversary of the Japanese Garden Research Society, this small front garden was crafted with materials carefully selected to produce the dignified, elegant atmosphere appropriate to Tsuruoka Hachiman-gu Shrine, a Kamakura-period structure. The designer used granite flagstones, chosen for beauty and ease of walking, for the pathway through the garden from the gate to the entrance of reception room. To the left of the entrance (when facing it from the outside) is a *tsukubai* arrangement containing a *kesa* stone basin in the Kamakura-period style. The front stone in the arrangement is in a distinctive V shape.

A prime feature of the garden, to the right of the entrance area, is the boat-shaped blue stone with its prominent prow. The tall stone is set off by a low bamboo branch fence, which represents the sea upon which the boat is floating. Part of the garden is bordered by a Kyoto-style Kenninji fence, topped by a cryptomeria bark screening fence.

· Front garden of the reception room: Stone Boat Garden

Design: Isao Yoshikawa. **Construction:** Shin'ichi Kosuge, Kazuo Ebihara, Ando Stone Materials; 1993. **Area:** 52.5 square meters. **Location:** Kamakura, Kanagawa Pref.

守永寺庭園
Shuei-ji Temple Garden

1. Der kleine Garten vom Erdgeschoß der Empfangshalle aus betrachtet. Von hier aus sieht man nicht, daß es noch ein Untergeschoß gibt.

2. *Cryptomeria* Sichtschutzzaun, Steinlaterne und Steinbecken.

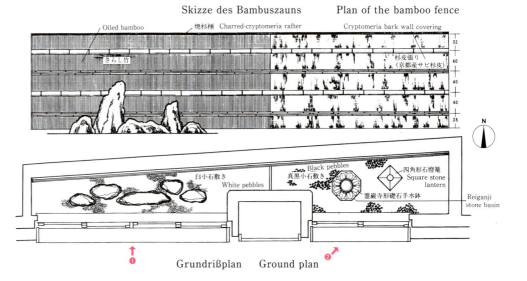

Kleiner Garten vor der Empfangshalle

Shuei-ji ist ein Tempel der „Pure Land" Sekte. Der Tempel hat eine unter dem Erdgeschoß liegende Empfangshalle, dessen kleiner Garten in zwei Hälften aufgeteilt ist. Zuerst verkleidete der Designer die Wände mit geflammtem, geöltem Bambus und einem *Cryptomeria* Sichtschutz als Zaunimitation. Vor der Bambuswand ist ein Arrangement aus fünf blauen Steinen in weißem Sand plaziert.

Gegenüber, vor dem Sichtschutz, befindet sich eine im Boden verankerte quadratische Steinlaterne sowie ein *Reiganji* Steinbecken; diese beiden Elemente stehen in einer mit kleinen schwarzen Steinen aufgeschütteten Fläche.

Innengarten: Garten des herabkommenden Amidas

Im Einklang mit den Lehren des „Pure Land" Buddhismus symbolisiert der Innengarten (zwischen der Haupt- und Empfangshalle) den herabkommenden Buddha *Amida*. Die Quelle dieses Designs waren zahlreiche Kunstgegenstände aus der *Kamakura* Periode. (Die Ankunft Amida amid, eines riesigen Buddhas, der jedes Leben beschützt).

客殿小庭・中庭〈来迎之庭〉
Small garden of the reception hall, Inner garden: Garden of the Descent of Amida

3. Der im Vordergrund stehende Stein verleiht dem Innengarten Perspektive.

4. Luftansicht auf die zwei „Wolken" des Innengartens.

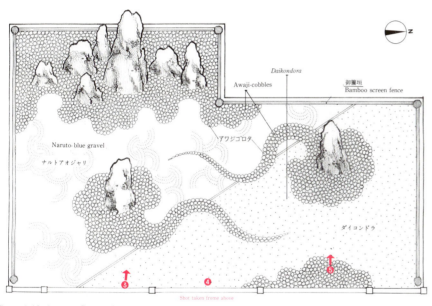

Grundrißplan   Ground plan

5. Blauer Stein, der *Kannon* repräsentiert.

Hier befindet sich *Amida* in Begleitung der beiden Bodhisattvas *Kannon* und *Seishi* (von zwei Steinen dargestellt). Sie stehen auf in Wolkenform angeordneten *Awaji* Kieselsteinen. Dahinter steht *Amida*, von mehreren Bodhisattvas umgeben. Zwei Hälften stellen einmal „Pure Land" (blauer Schotter) und unsere Welt dar (*Dwarf Snake's Beard*). Der Bambus-Sichtschutzzaun rund um den Garten vervollständigt die Schaffung des „Pure Land".

Small garden of the reception hall

Shuei-ji is a temple of the Pure Land sect. The temple has a reception hall located below ground level, whose small garden, divided into two sections, doubles as a skylight. Designing such a small garden proved challenging, but provided lessons that may be valuable for others attempting to do something creative with limited space. First, the designer covered the walls with charred, oiled bamboo and cryptomeria bark, in imitation of fences. In front of the bamboo wall is an arrangement of five blue stones set in white pebbles. Opposite this, in front of the bark wall, is a square stone lantern implanted in the ground and a Reiganji stone basin; these are set in an area of small black stones.

Inner garden: Garden of the Descent of Amida

In line with the doctrines of Pure Land Buddhism, the inner garden (located between the temple's main hall and reception room) was designed to symbolize the descent of the buddha Amida. The source for this design was the numerous pieces of Kamakura-period artwork depicting this event—the coming of Amida amid a multitude of buddhas to save all living beings. Here, two bodhisattvas in Amida's retinue, Kannon and Seishi, are represented by single stones; they sit on Awaji cobblestones arranged in the shape of clouds. Behind them is a stone arrangement representing Amida himself, surrounded by several additional bodhisattvas. The garden is cut in two diagonally, the Pure Land side covered with blue gravel and the side representing the present world planted with dwarf snake's beard. The colors are a beautiful combination. The bamboo screen fence around the garden completes the creation of a "pure land."

1. The small garden viewed from the basement-level reception hall. There is no sense of being underground.
2. Cryptomeria bark "fence," stone lantern, and stone basin.
3. The standing stone in the foreground gives the inner garden a sense of perspective.
4. Aerial view of the two "clouds" of the inner garden.
5. Blue stone representing Kannon.

· Small garden of the reception hall & Inner garden: Garden of the Descent of Amida
Design: Isao Yoshikawa. **Construction:** Shin'ichi Kosuge, Kazuo Ebihara; 1994. **Area:** 7 square meters. **Location:** Ichihara, Chiba Pref.

新藤邸庭園
The Shindo Home Garden

1. Trockenes Flußbett, von einer Steinbrücke überspannt.

2. Gartenansicht des Vorgartens vom Haupteingang in Richtung Haus.

3. Ein Fußweg aus einzelnen Platten führt zum zweiten Eingang des Hauses.

1. Dry streambed, crossed by a stone bridge.
2. The portion of the garden in front of the main entrance to the house serves as a front garden.
3. Stepping stones leading to the house's second entrance.
4. The cycad and blue stones of this crane stone arrangement are well balanced.

〈潜龍庭〉
Senryu-tei garden

Die trocken angelegte Landschaft des Gartens im Osten des Hauses "Shindo home" wurde auf einem langen Grundstück, das sich von Norden nach Süden erstreckt, angelegt. Zwei Fußwege durchqueren den Vor- und Hauptgarten. Um eine Einheit zu erhalten, wurde ein 40 Meter langes trockenes Flußbett mit ins Design aufgenommen. Das Flußbett kann auch (wegen seiner Form) als Drache gesehen werden. Drachen gelten als traditionelle Bewacher des Ostens (der Name des Gartens Senryu-tei bedeutet „verborgener Drache").

Der Haupteingang des Hauses (am rechten Ende des Steinwegs) liegt ein wenig höher als das Eingangstor an der Straße. Deshalb baute der Designer einen leicht ansteigenden Fußweg ohne Stufen. Die wunderschöne japanische Rot-Pinie wurde, schon lange bevor der Garten gebaut wurde, direkt am Haupteingang gepflanzt. Jetzt ist sie der Mittelpunkt des Schildkröten-Arrangements und gibt dem Garten die nötige Tiefe.

Das Hauptziel für diesen Garten war, einen zusammenhängenden, wunderschönen Ausblick vom im japanischen Stil eingerichteten Zeichenraum zu erreichen. Ein im Stil eines indischen Tintengemäldes aussehendes Steinarrangement wurde aufgestellt, um den Brunnen vor dem Fenster dieses Raums zu verbergen. Dahinter wurde eine Bergkette als sogenannte „Ferne Hügel" Formation aufgebaut. Rechts daneben ist ein trockener Wasserfall, die „Quelle" des trockenen Flußbetts.

Eine wunderschön geformte Cyade wächst genau links neben dem Eingangstor. Um eine gute Übersicht vom Wohnzimmer des Hauses zu erhalten, wurde ein Kranich-Steinarrangement um den Baum herum angelegt. Die verschiedenen Arten der Fußwege sind durch die Aufnahmen und Diagramme gut zu erkennen.

4. Die Cyade und die blauen Steine dieses Arrangements sind sehr schön aufeinander abgestimmt.

Schildkröteninsel

Japanische Gärten sind bekannt dafür, aus Tradition Formationen einzubauen, die z.B. Schildkröten- und Kranich-Insel genannt werden. Diese auf chinesische Legenden zurückgehende Formationen sind ein Teil der Mystik Horais, dem Land des ewigen Lebens. Beide symbolisieren den Wunsch nach einem langen Leben, die Schildkröten-Formation hat die ältere Tradition der beiden Arten. Die dargestellte Schildkröte ist tatsächlich die mysteriöse „Goo" Meeresschildkröte, die besser bekannt ist unter dem Namen Riesen-Meeresschildkröte. Es wurde gesagt, daß sich Mount Horai auf dem Schildkröten-Rücken erheben würde. Das Steinarrangement stellt nicht die Schildkröte im Wasser dar.

Deshalb wird in der Tradition des Gartenbaus die Schildkröteninsel nicht gebaut, um wirklich eine Schildkröte darzustellen. Vielmehr soll dadurch deren Kraft, Mysteriosität und Originalität dargestellt werden (dazu ist natürlich Originalität des Künstlers gefordert). Eine Schildkröte, die zu realistisch aussieht, oder die entsprechende Ausdruckskraft nicht erreicht, kann den Wert des Gartens nur vermindern (Yoshikawa).

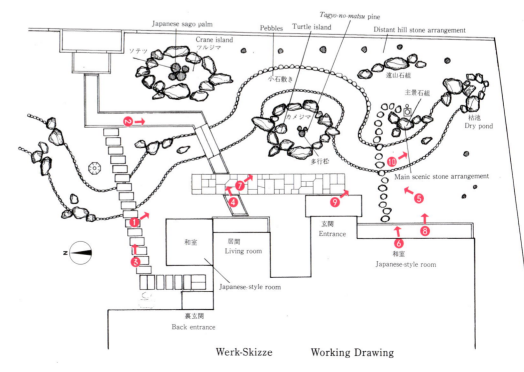

Werk-Skizze Working Drawing

〈潜龍庭〉
Senryu-tei garden

5. Japanische Rot-Pinie und ein Teil des Schildkröten-Arrangements.

6. Trockenes Flußbett mit Steinarrangement vom Salon des Hauses aus betrachtet. Der Steinweg führt zu einem Brunnen.

7. Fußweg aus Platten und Schildkröten-Arrangement.

5. Japanese red pine, part of a turtle stone arrangement.
6. Dry streambed and stone arrangements as viewed from the parlor of the house. The stepping stones lead to a well.
7. Cut-stone path and turtle stone arrangement.
8. India ink painting stone arrangement and distant-mountain stone beyond it.
9. View of the garden with mountain range stone arrangement in the distance.
10. Dry-waterfall stone arrangement that serves as the "source" of the dry streambed.

• Senryu-tei
Design: Isao Yoshikawa. **Construction:** Shin'ichi Kosuge, Kazuo Ebihara, Ando Stone Materials; 1992. **Area:** 390 square meters. **Location:** Ichihara, Chiba Pref.

〈潜龍庭〉
Senryu-tei garden

The dry-landscape garden of the Shindo home is laid out on a long piece of land extending from north to south on the eastern side of the house. Two paths cross the garden from the outer gate to the house's two entranceways; the garden thus serves as a front garden as well as the home's main garden. To provide a sense a unity, a long (forty meters) dry streambed was included in the design. The streambed can also be considered as representing a dragon, the traditional guardian of the east (the name given to the garden by the designer, Senryu-tei, means "hidden-dragon garden").

The main entrance to the house (at the right end of the cut-stone path shown in the accompanying diagram) is somewhat higher than the outer gate to the street, so the designer used a sloping path, without steps, to connect them. A beautiful Japanese red pine planted at the main entrance well before we laid out the garden was preserved and now serves as the focal point of a turtle stone arrangement. The dry streambed curves behind this arrangement, giving the garden a sense of depth.

One design goal for this garden was to provide a coherent, pleasing view outside the Japanese-style drawing room (on the right side of the diagram). An india ink painting stone arrangement was positioned to hide the well in front of the window of this room, and a mountain range stone arrangement, including a so-called distant-mountain stone, was placed beyond this. To the right of this is a dry waterfall, the "source" of the garden's dry streambed.

A beautifully shaped cycad was growing just inside the garden gate, to the left. To provide a pleasant view from the living room of the house (on the left side of the diagram), a crane stone arrangement was set up around the tree. The several styles of paths are seen in the accompanying diagram and photographs.

On Turtle Islands

Japanese gardens have traditionally been fond of the use of formations called "turtle islands" and "crane islands." These originated in Chinese legend, it is thought, and are part of the myth of Horai, the land of eternal life. Both symbolize the wish for longevity, the turtle being the far older tradition of the two.

The turtle which is represented is in fact the mysterious Goo turtle of the sea, which is also known as the giant snapping turtle. Mt. Horai was said to rise over this turtle's back. The formation does not represent a turtle in a pond or swamp.

Therefore, in the tradition of garden-building, a turtle island is not constructed to resemble an actual turtle, but rather by definition to express strength, mystery and originality - and this is where the artist's originality is required. A turtle which looks too realistic, or which fails to exert adequate power, can only reduce the value of the garden. (Yoshikawa)

8. Steinarrangement mit indischer Tinte bemalt und dahinter der „Ferne Hügel" Stein.

9. Gartenansicht mit Bergketten-Arrangement im Hintergrund.

10. Trockener Wasserfall, der als „Quelle" des trockenen Flußbetts dient.

岩井邸庭園
The Iwai Home Garden

1. Blick auf den Hauptgarten vom Haus aus gesehen. Die Brücke und die Halbinseln schaffen die nötige Tiefe im Garten.

2. Trockener Wasserfall aus blauen Steinen im hinteren Teil des Gartens.

1. View of the main garden from the house. The bridge and peninsulas create a sense of depth.
2. Dry waterfall arrangement of blue stones in the rear of the garden.
3. Small stone lantern and Kinkakuji fence in the background.
4. Two-stone arrangement on the tip of a peninsula; the ground cover is *kokumazasa* bamboo grass.

主庭
Main garden

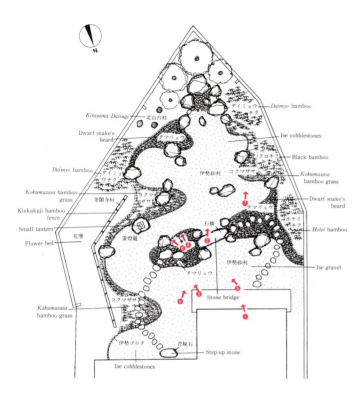

Grundrißplan   Ground plan

3. Kleine Steinlaterne und ein *Kinkakuji* Zaun im Hintergrund.

4. Zwei-Stein-Arrangement auf der Spitze einer Halbinsel; der Boden ist mit *Kokumazasa* Bambusgras bepflanzt.

Wie auf dem beigefügten Grundrißplan zu sehen, ist das Grundstück des Hauptgartens ziemlich untypisch geformt. Dies erforderte eine sorgfältige Planung, was schließlich ein sehr interessantes Layout ergab. Ergebnis ist eine vom Besitzer gewünschte trockene Landschaft aus Bambus und Stein-Arrangements aus Chlorit-Schist-Steinen.

Ein trockener Teich nimmt sehr viel Platz in Anspruch; der erhabene Effekt wird durch fünf Halbinseln rings um den Teich erzielt. Eine der Halbinseln ist durch eine Brücke mit der Insel in der Teichmitte verbunden, die sich genau vor einem der Räume des Hauses befindet. Obwohl es nicht üblich ist, ein Objekt dieser Art direkt vor dem Gebäude zu erbauen, bringt der hintere linke Stein als Brückenpfeiler die gewünschte Perspektive. Die Insel ist auf der anderen Seite des Teichs durch einen Steinweg mit dem Festland verbunden. Eine kleine quadratische Steinlaterne auf einem abgeflachten Stein links hinter der Insel rundet den Blick aus dem Wohnzimmer ab. Der trockene Wasserfall befindet sich im hinteren Teil des Teichs in der Spitze des Gartens.

Im Garten finden sich verschiedene Pflanzenarten: immergrüne Sorten wie Bayberries und Kamelien hinter dem Wasserfall, verschiedene Arten Bambus, *Kokumazasa* Bambusgras und *Dwarf Snake's Beard* als Bodenabdeckung sowie Beete mit japanischen Blumen. Der Besitzer des *Iwai* Anwesens bat den Designer, ein *Tsukubai* Arrangement im Vorgarten des Hauses zu gestalten, der schon fertig angelegt war.

Im Zentrum des Arrangements ist ein *Kasa* Steinbecken, das aus einem Teil des Daches einer *Stupa* gemacht war; das Dach wurde umgedreht und ein Becken daraus geformt. In diesem Fall wurde ein *Stupa* aus der frühen Edo-Periode hergenommen. Das Becken ruht auf einem Zylinder, und ein großer felsenförmiger Chlorit-Shist-Stein bietet einen starken Hintergrund. Der Stein im Vordergrund und die Steine des Fußwegs, vom Garteneingang zum Haus führt, sind aus *Diorit*. Ein *suikinkutsu* wurde neben dem Eingang gefunden, das jetzt einen angenehmen Klang für die Bewohner und Gäste verbreitet.

As the accompanying diagram indicates, the land on which the main garden of the Iwai home is situated is of a rather unusual shape, requiring careful planning but resulting in an interesting layout. The owner desired a dry-landscape garden with stone arrangements and bamboo. The stone arrangements employ chlorite-schist stones.

A dry pond takes up much of the space in the garden; a majestic effect was created by including five peninsulas in the outline of the pond. One of the peninsulas is joined to an island in the middle of the pond by a stone bridge, which sits almost directly in front of one of the rooms of the house. Although it is not usual to put an object in front of a building in this fashion, the tall bridge accessory stone to the left rear of the bridge creates the necessary sense of perspective. The island is connected to the other side of the pond by a stepping stone path. A small, square stone lantern placed on a flat-topped stone to the left of and behind the island helps unify the view from the living room of the house. A dry waterfall arrangement appears at the rear of the pond, at the apex of the garden.

There are a variety of plants in the garden: evergreens such as bayberries and camellias behind the dry waterfall, several kinds of bamboo, *kokumazasa* bamboo grass and dwarf snake's beard for ground cover, and a bed of flowers native to Japan.

主庭
Main garden

5. Östliche Sektion des Gartens.

6. Steinbrücke und Steinarrangement.

7. Großer Stein, der die Stärke des Trockenteichufers darstellt.

8. Kleine Steinlaterne. Die vier Füße stehen für Stabilität.

The owner of the Iwai property asked the designer to create a *tsukubai* arrangement for the house's front garden, which was already otherwise complete. At the center of the arrangement is a *kasa* stone basin, which is made from the roof section of a stupa; the roof is turned upside down and a basin is carved out of it. In this case, an early Edo-period stupa was used. The basin rests on a cylindrical base, and a large mountain-shaped chlorite-schist rear stone provides a strong background. The arrangement's front stone and the steppingstones leading from the entrance to the house are of diorite. A *suikinkutsu* is found underground near the entrance, creating a pleasant sound for the residents and their guests.

5. Eastern section of the garden.
6. Stone bridge and stone arrangements.
7. Large stone, adding a sense of strength to the edge of the dry pond.
8. Small stone lantern. The four feet provide a sense of stability.
9. *Tsukubai* arrangement in the front garden, with a mountain-shaped blue stone in the rear.
10. Stone basin, taken from the top of an early Edo-period stupa.

前庭
Front garden

9. *Tsukubai* Arrangement im Vorgarten, mit einem blauen Stein mit Hügelform im Hintergrund.

Gartenelemente

Die Erscheinung von Steinlaternen und Stein-Wasserbecken in Gärten geht bis in die frühe *Edo* Periode zurück und zeigt den Einfluß der Teehaus-Gärten.

Wenn man diese Elemente im Garten verwendet, gilt es, gewisse Regeln einzuhalten: wird eine Steinlaterne angebracht, darf es nicht irgendeine sein, sondern allein als Kunstwerk stehen können. Um ein wertvolles Stück zu erkennen, muß man mehrere Kunstwerke betrachten, um den Unterschied festzustellen. Auf jeden Fall sollte man auf billige Massenproduktion verzichten.

Die Zahl der wirklich fähigen Steinmetze in Japan wird zusehens kleiner und deshalb steigt die Nachfrage nach Produkten aus China und Korea. Leider hat die große Nachfrage nach Kopien zu schlechteren Anfertigungen geführt, und nur noch wenige Stücke können als sehr gut bezeichnet werden. Ich bemühe mich immer, eine exakte Nachbildung zu fertigen und verwende nur die bestmögliche Technik für diese Gegenstände (Yoshikawa).

10. Steinbecken, aus einem *Stupa* aus der frühen *Edo* Periode.

Design: Isao Yoshikawa. **Construction:** Shin'ichi Kosuge, Kazuo Ebihara, Ando Stone Materials; 1992. **Area:** 390 square meters. **Location:** Sakura, Chiba Pref.

榎本邸庭園
The Enomoto Home Garden

1. Trockenes Flußbett mit einem Zaun aus Bambuszweigen, in alter Weise erbaut (links). „Quelle" ist ein trockener Wasserfall, der weiter hinten zu sehen ist.

Der Besitzer des *Enmoto Homes*, ein Blumen-Designer, wollte seinen Garten im Einklang mit der Natur gestaltet haben. Der Designer entschied sich zuerst für ein Arrangement aus dem modernen Gartenbau, das das Konzept der *Heian* Periode („Pathos of things" – mono-no-aware) widerspiegelt. Das Hauptmerkmal des Gartens ist ein trockenes Flußbett. In der Mitte des Gartens befindet sich ein Bambuszweigzaun im alten Stil, den man auf vielen Bildern der *Heian*- und *Kamakura* Periode wiederfindet. Der Zaun wurde gebaut, indem man 5–8 Stangen des *Mosobambus* als Stützpfeiler zusammenband und sie dann gegeneinander aufstellte (siehe Bild 6). Wilde Chrysanthemen und andere Blumen wachsen sehr gut in solchen Zäunen. Um eine gewisse Trennung zu erhalten, wurden dunkelblaue Chlorit-Schist-Steine verwendet. Entlang des trockenen Flußbetts sind Steinarrangements eingebaut worden.

Ein weiteres Gestaltungsziel für diesen Garten war, ihn mit dem Baustil des Hauses in Einklang zu bringen. Das Wohnzimmer ist durch eine aus schmalen Baumstämmen gefertigte Veranda umrandet; darunter befindet sich ein Streifen aus großen Kieselsteinen, in an mehreren Stellen Scheiben eines *Cryptomeria* Stamms eingelassen sind; der größte davon ist gleich am Haus eingelassen, um das Betreten der Veranda zu erleichtern. Die Fläche vor dem im japanischen Stil eingerichteten Raums ist wie ein Teegarten angelegt. Dabei ist ein *Tsukubai* Arrangement über die Mitte eines *Teppatsu* Steinbeckens ausgerichtet. Der vordere Stein dieses Arrangements ist aus *Diorit*.

2. *Sanzon*, trockener Wasserfall aus blauen Chlorit-Schist-Steinen.

3. *Tsukubai* Arrangement.

1. Dry streambed, with an old-style bamboo branch fence to the left. The "source" is a dry waterfall in the distance.
2. *Sanzon* dry-waterfall arrangement of blue chlorite-schist stones.
3. *Tsukubai* arrangement.
4. Upstream portion of the dry streambed. The stone arrangements emphasize the curved lines.
5. The "wave-dividing" stone in the middle of the stream adds a touch of interest.

榎本邸庭園
The Enomoto Home Garden

4. Ein Blick flußaufwärts. Das Steinarrangement betont den kurvenreichen Verlauf.

5. Der „Wellenstein" in der Mitte des Flusses weckt Interesse.

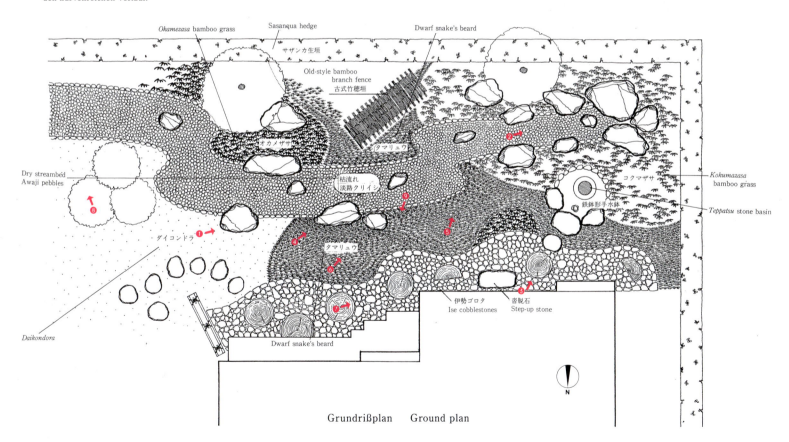

Grundrißplan   Ground plan

The owner of the Enomoto home, a teacher of flower arrangement, wanted his garden designed in line with his love for natural scenery. The designer decided upon an arrangement that would use modern garden layout principles to reflect the Heian-period literary concept of the "pathos of things" (*mono-no-aware*). The central feature of the garden is a dry streambed. In the center of the garden is an old-style bamboo branch fence of the type seen in many Heian- and Kamakura-period picture scrolls. The fence was constructed by bundling together into support poles five to eight stalks of *moso* bamboo and leaning these against each other, as seen in Figure 6. Wild chrysanthemums and other flowers growing in such a fence add to its rusticity. To avoid any sense of gaudiness, dark blue chlorite-schist stones were used in the garden, and the stone arrangements were positioned in accordance with the lines of the dry streambed.

An additional goal in the design of this garden was to have it harmonize with the mountain villa style of the house. The living room is edged by a narrow veranda of logs; below this was placed a strip of Ise cobblestones in which several cross sections of a cryptomeria trunk were inlaid, the large one nearest the door positioned to help people step onto the veranda. The area in front of a Japanese-style room of the house is arranged like a tea ceremony garden, with a *tsukubai* arrangement centered on a *teppatsu* stone basin. The front stone of the arrangement is of diorite.

榎本邸庭園
The Enomoto Home Garden

6. Bambuszweigzaun, im alten Stil erbaut.

6. Old-style bamboo branch fence.
7. Curved path of Ise cobblestones.
8. *Shishiodoshi* (bamboo device that fills with then releases water, making an echoing sound against a rock as it drops back to position).
9. Cobblestone path and cross sections of cryptomeria trunk.

Design: Isao Yoshikawa. **Construction:** Ando Stone Materials; 1985. **Area:** 60 square meters. **Location:** Ichihara, Chiba Pref.

7. Kurviger Fußweg aus großen Kieselsteinen.

8. *Shishiodoshi* (Bambusrohr als Klangkörper).

9. Kieselsteinweg und Zweige aus *Cryptomeria*.

岩田邸庭園
The Iwata Home Garden

1. Blick auf den Garten aus dem zweiten Stock des Hauses.
   View of the garden from the second floor of the house.

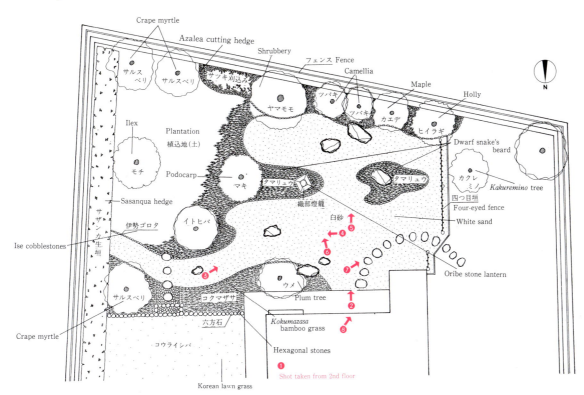

Grundrißplan   Ground plan

岩田邸庭園
The Iwata Home Garden

2. Ansicht aus dem ersten Stock, die *Oribe* Steinlaterne bildet das Zentrum des Gartens.

3. Trockenes Flußbett und *Oribe* Laterne.

4. Felseninsel mit Bergmassiv als zusätzlicher Blickpunkt ganz rechts oben.

Das im japanischen Stil erbaute *Iwata* Home ist auf einem erhöhten Grundstück angelegt. Da der Garten sich in der Höhe des zweiten Stockwerks der umliegenden Häuser befindet, wurden eine Azaleen-Hecke und andere Pflanzen entlang des Zauns gepflanzt. Der Garten selbst ist als Trockenlandschaft angelegt. Er besteht aus zwei Hälften. Die eine beinhaltet den trockenen Teich mit von links in den Teich einschneidenden Halbinseln. Der Teich ist mit weißem Sand (*Mikawa-Shirakawa*) aus der *Gifu* Präfektur ausgefüllt. Der exakt geschnittene Granit als Grenze des Teichs zum Festland ist in wunderschönen Kurven besonders an den Spitzen der Halbinsel sehr sauber ausgelegt. Eine restaurierte *Oribe* Steinlaterne aus der frühen Edo-Periode ist genau in der Mitte des Gartens auf einer Halbinsel aufgestellt. Dies ist eine der ersten Laternen im *Oribe* Stil. Ein *Sanzon* Steinarrangement, das Hauptmerkmal des Gartens, verbindet den Teich mit der Halbinsel und vereint gleichzeitig die Ebene mit den dreidimensionalen Teilen des Arrangements. In der linken Hälfte des Gartens, angeschlossen an den trockenen Teich, wurde ein trockenes Flußbett als zusätzlicher Blickpunkt angelegt. Die Anlage beinhaltet relativ wenig Steine, die aber sehr gut verteilt wurden und somit schöne Effekte und natürliche Perspektiven erzielen. Vom Hause aus erblickt man im Vordergrund ein Arrangement aus zwei Steinen und *Kokumazasa* Bambusgras, die Steinlaterne erhebt sich in der Mitte des Gartens und das *Sanzon* Arrangement ist im Hintergrund zu sehen.

Design: Isao Yoshikawa. **Construction:** Ando Stone Materials, Mitsuhashi Garden Design; 1986. **Area:** 104 square meters. **Location:** Nagareyama, Chiba Pref.

岩田邸庭園
The Iwata Home Garden

5. *Sanzon* Steinarrangement, mit Begleitstein rechts neben der Insel und weiteren Steinen im trockenen Teich.

6. Restaurierte *Oribe* Laterne aus der frühen *Edo* Periode.

7. Zaun aus vier Pfählen und Tor zum Gemüsegarten rechts.

8. Fußweg aus Steinen, der zum Tor des Gemüsegartens führt.

The Iwata home, constructed in the traditional Japanese style, is located on an area of high ground. Because the garden is on about the same level as the second stories of the surrounding houses, an azalea hedge and other plants appear on the boundary. Otherwise, the garden is in the dry-landscape style, with a basic division into two parts (see accompanying diagram) including a dry pond to the right, containing pure Mikawa-Shirakawa white sand from Gifu Prefecture, and a peninsular piece of land jutting into the pond from the left. The border is delineated by granite cut very finely to create beautiful curved lines, especially that of the tip of the peninsula.

An early-Edo *oribe* stone lantern restored by the writer has been placed in the very center of the garden, on the peninsula; this is the earliest style of *oribe* lantern in existence. A *sanzon* stone arrangement, the focal point of the garden, spans the island in the dry pond and the area of the pond behind it, enhancing the balance between the flatness of the garden and its three-dimensional features. On the left side of the garden, connected to the dry pond, is a dry streambed that, along with the rocks placed in it, adds interest to the layout. The garden contains relatively few stone arrangements, but employs them to good effect, creating a sense of perspective: seen from the window of the house, a two-stone arrangement and *kokumazasa* bamboo grass are nearby, the stone lantern appears to be in the middle distance, and the *sanzon* arrangement looks farther away.

2. Viewed from a window on the first floor, the *oribe* lantern forms the centerpiece of the garden.
3. Dry streambed and *oribe* lantern.
4. The mountain-shaped rock island in the upper right adds interest to the layout.
5. *Sanzon* stone arrangement, with the accessory stone on the right side on the island and the other stones in the dry pond.
6. Restored early-Edo *oribe* lantern.
7. "Four-eyed" fence and gate setting off a vegetable garden to the right.
8. Stepping stones leading to the gate to the vegetable garden.

渡辺邸庭園
The Watanabe Home Garden

1. Trockener Teich mit Wasserfallarrangement ganz hinten links.

2. Das *Watanabe Home* mit einer Mauer umgeben. Der Garten ist hinter der Mauer rechts angelegt.

Skizze   Sketch

〈静寿園〉
Seiju-en garden

3. Fußweg aus Steinen durch Haarmoos.

4. Die rechte Seite des Gartens mit Blick auf die Schildkröteninsel.

5. Grotten-Steinarrangement. Der große Stein links ist Teil des *Yin-Yang* Glaubens.

Das *Watanabe Home* geht bis in die *Meiji* Zeit zurück, als der Garten vor einem der hinteren Zimmer einen kleinen Teich hatte. Später wurde der Garten dann erweitert, eine Mauer um den Garten gezogen und somit ein komplett neues Aussehen geschaffen. Der Garten wurde in einer Trockenlandschaft angelegt und enthält sowohl verschiedene Elemente aus dem alten Garten als auch neue Stein-Arrangements. Der ursprüngliche Teich wurde umfunktioniert und zu einem trockenen Teich erweitert. Die darin bestehende Schildkröteninsel wurde erhalten. Hinter dem Teich weiter links wurde ein trockener Wasserfall aus heimischen Steinen als Hauptmerkmal des Gartens angelegt. Genau gegenüber des Wasserfalls ist eine Grotte aufgebaut. Diese verleiht dem Garten nicht nur etwas Geheimnisvolles, sondern auch visuelle Tiefe. Die Grotte symbolisiert die Steinhütten, in denen uralte Bergwizards leben, und steht gleichzeitig für Langlebigkeit – eine sehr gute Eigenschaft für die Klinik, die die Familie *Watanabe* besitzt. Die verschiedenen Gartenelemente stammen aus der *Horai* Zeit, wonach in der chinesischen Legende uralte Wizzards in den Bergen leben.

The Watanabe home dates from the Meiji era, at which time the garden, facing one of the back rooms of the house, had a small pond. More recently, the garden was expanded and an earthen wall built around it, so a complete revamping was undertaken. The new garden is laid out in the dry-landscape style and includes several stone arrangements, as well as some elements of the old garden.

The original pond was drained and converted to a dry pond, with its original turtle island retained. Behind the pond and to the left a dry-waterfall arrangement, the central feature of the garden, was laid out with local stones. Offsetting the waterfall on the right side of the garden is a grotto stone arrangement. Besides adding mystery and visual depth to the garden, the arrangement is representative of the stone huts in which legendary ageless mountain wizards lived and, as such, is a symbol of longevity appropriate to the medical clinic run by the Watanabe family. The various garden elements result in what can be termed a Horai style, after the mountain in Chinese legend on which ageless wizards lived.

1. Dry pond, with waterfall arrangement at the far left.
2. The Watanabe home, surrounded by an earthen wall. The garden is behind the wall to the right.
3. Stepping stones amid hair moss.
4. Right side of the garden, with a view of the turtle island.
5. Grotto stone arrangement. The tall stone at the left is part of the yin-yang symbolism.

〈静寿園〉
Seiju-en garden

6. Wasserfall-Steinarrangement; der große Stein links strahlt Stärke aus.

7. Fußweg, der links zur Grotte führt.

8. Steinbrücke im trockenen Teich.

9. Gesamtanblick des Gartens. Der Stein im Teich unten links ist ein Wellenstein und Teil des Wasserfalls.

6. Waterfall stone arrangement; the large accessory stone on the left adds emphasis.
7. Stepping stones to the left of the grotto arrangement.
8. Stone bridge in the dry pond.
9. Overall view of the garden. The stone in the pond in the lower left is a stream-dividing stone, part of the waterfall arrangement.

· Seiju-en garden
Design: Isao Yoshikawa. **Construction:** Ohmachi Shuho Gardens; 1994. **Area:** 269 square meters. **Location:** Fukuchiyama, Kyoto Pref.

矢数邸庭園
The Yakazu Home Garden

坪庭
Indoor garden

1. Der Garten vom Eingang des Hauses aus betrachtet. Im Vordergrund ist ein *Kinkakuji* Zaun.
The garden viewed from the entrance to the house. In the foreground is a Kinkakuji fence.

Der Innengarten des *Yakazu Homes,* eines Betongebäudes mitten in Tokyo, wurde als Miniatur-Landschaft neben dem Eingangsbereich angelegt. Der Garten befindet sich an einer dunklen Stelle unter dem Treppenhaus. Während solche Voraussetzungen es normalerweise nicht erlauben, einen Garten zu gestalten, ist es für den japanischen Gartenbau kein Problem, solche dunklen Plätze auszubauen. Schlichtes Design kombiniert mit wenig Material ist der Schlüssel zum Erfolg. Hier wurden die Wände mit langen Bambusstangen, diagonal angelegt, verkleidet und mit zwei Kunstwerken auf dem Boden vollendet: ein Steinbecken aus der späten *Kamakura* Periode, gefertigt aus *Hokyointo Stupa,* sowie eine kleine Steinlaterne, die auf Steinpodest gestellt wurde. Der Boden ist ganz einfach mit Schotter bedeckt.

2. Der Bambuszaun an den Wänden erinnert an fliegende Pfeile und ist an den Familiennamen *ya* (Pfeil) angelehnt.
The bamboo fence against the walls is an abstract representation of arrows flying, based on the *ya* ("arrow") of the family's surname.

The inner garden of the Yakazu home, a concrete building located in the middle of Tokyo, is laid out on a miniature piece of land near the entrance to the house. The garden also happens to be located in a dark area under a stairwell. While these conditions might cause homeowners to resign themselves to not having a garden, the principles of Japanese gardening permit the effective use of such space. A simple design using a minimum of materials is the key to success. Here, the walls have been covered with long pieces of bamboo, emphasizing the diagonal direction, and two pieces of artwork were placed on the floor of the garden itself: a stone basin made from a late-Kamakura period *hokyointo* stupa and a small stone lantern of the writer's design placed on a pedestal stone. The garden floor is covered uncomplicatedly with gravel.

· Inner Garden
Design: Isao Yoshikawa. **Construction:** Aoyama Landscaping; 1983. **Area:** 4.86 square meters. **Location:** Shinjuku-ku, Tokyo

医院庭園〈仙海之庭〉
Clinic garden: Senkai no Niwa

1. Die verschiedenen Elemente dieses Gartens trennen diese Welt vom Stadtleben.

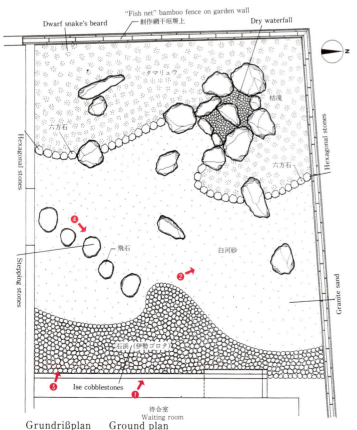

Grundrißplan / Ground plan

Dr. Yakazu führt eine bekannte Klinik für traditionelle chinesische Medizin. In dieser Klinik ist auch seine Wohnung untergebracht. Ein kleiner Garten aus einer Trockenlandschaft wurde vor dem Wartezimmer angelegt. Das Hauptziel bei der Planung des Gartens war, ihn vom Umfeld abzuschirmen, da das Gebäude von vielen zweistöckigen Häusern umgeben ist. Deshalb wurde auf die Gartenmauer ein Fischnetz-Zaun (den Trockenzäunen der Fischer am Meer nachempfunden) gebaut, der von einem Stahlskelett gestützt wird. Obwohl die Wand zwischen dem Garten und dem Wartezimmer mit Fenstern durchzogen ist, könnten sitzende Patienten nur den Zaun und die Spitzen der verschiedenen Gartenelemente sehen. Deshalb wurde eine leicht ansteigende Landschaft erbaut. Die aufgefüllten Elemente wurden durch sechseckige Steinpfähle befestigt. Das Hauptmerkmal dieser erhöhten Anlage ist ein trockener Wasserfall aus blauen Chlorit-Schist-Steinen. Der Boden des Gartens am Gebäude ist mit großen Kieselsteinen bedeckt und läßt so einen Steinstrand vermuten; der Anblick hier wurde von außerhalb des Gebäudes aufgenommen. Einem Gemälde aus indischer Tinte nachempfunden, wurde dieser Garten im *Horai* Stil erbaut. Er spiegelt Meeresszenen wider und symbolisiert Langlebigkeit – angepaßt an die Heilmethoden des Arztes.

医院庭園〈仙海之庭〉
Clinic garden: Senkai no Niwa

1. The various elements of this garden make it into a world separate from its urban surroundings.
2. "Fish net" bamboo fence.
3. Stepping stones and rock island in a dry pond of Ise gravel.
4. Sandbar-shaped "stony beach." The stepping stones lead to an air-conditioning unit.

2. Fischnetz-Bambuszaun.

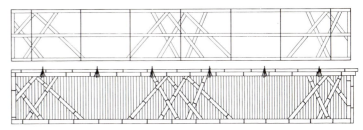

Fischnetz-Bambuszaun   Plan of the "fish net" bamboo fence

3. Fußweg aus Steinen und Felseninsel in einem trockenen Teich aus Schotter.

4. Steinstrand. Der Fußweg führt zu den klimatisierten Räumen.

Dr. Yakazu runs a well-known clinic of traditional Chinese medicine located in the same building as his home. A small dry-landscape garden is situated outside the clinic's waiting room. The most important considerations in the design of this garden were the need to screen the garden from the surroundings (the building happens to be located in an area of town with a large number of two-story print shops) and the relationship between the garden and the waiting room. To solve the first problem, the designer placed a "fish net" bamboo fence (imitative of fishers' nets drying on the seashore) atop the garden wall, supported by a steel skeleton.

Although the wall between the garden and waiting room is lined with windows, patients seated in the waiting room would be able to seen only the fence and the top portion of any garden elements. Thus, the designer filled in the portion of the garden floor opposite the windows and against the outer wall, holding the soil in place with hexagonal upright support stones. The primary feature of this raised section is a bi-level dry-waterfall arrangement of blue chlorite-schist stones. The floor of the section of the lower portion of the garden against the building is covered with Ise cobblestones, representative of a stony beach; the emphasis here was on the view from outside the property.

Laid out in imitation of an india ink painting, the garden is in a Horai style (see p. 49) that emphasizes scenes from the sea and symbolizes a theme, longevity, appropriate to the doctor's practice.

Gartenthemen

Der japanische Garten ist nicht nur eine Zierde für ein Gebäude; in seiner Form und Ausführung sollte man auch die spirituelle Schönheit sehen. Der wichtigste Punkt ist ein Hauptthema. Es gibt sehr viele verschiedene Themen, von schlicht bis schwer, und alle sind unterschiedlich. Für Wohnhäuser verwendet man meist schlichte Themen, während man in Tempel- oder Sektengärten häufig originalgetreue Einblicke findet.

Jedoch, ganz gleich wie originalgetreu das Konzept auch ist, wenn sich das Grundstück nicht eignet, ist die ganze Arbeit umsonst. Und hier beginnt die eigentliche Arbeit des Landschaftsbaus.

Das Thema wird in den ersten Schritten der Gartenplanung festgelegt, doch auch wenn der fertige Garten davon abweicht, so hat der Designer im Sinne des Betrachters gehandelt und die Schönheit des Gartens damit unterstrichen (Yoshikawa).

- **Clinic Garden:** Senkai no Niwa
Design: Isao Yoshikawa. **Construction:** Aoyama Landscaping; 1983. **Area:** 27.5 square meters. **Location:** Shinjuku-ku, Tokyo

鬼石町翠嶺庭
Onishi-machi Suirei-tei Garden

1. Die Steinarrangements sind streng und unüblich – schaffen jedoch die Anlehnung an ein Gemälde aus indischer Tinte.

Suirei-tei ist einer von vielen kleinen Stadtgärten, die von *Onishi* geschaffen wurden, um die heimischen quaderförmigen Chlorit-Schist-Steine darzustellen. Durch den kleinen *Tumulus* im Hintergrund wirkt dieses Arrangement zusätzlich interessant. Der Designer baute einen *Sanzon* Wasserfall am oberen Ende des Gartens. Dort entspringt ein trockener Fluß. Der große, dicke Stein wurde genau in der Mitte des Arrangements plaziert und gegen den Flußverlauf ausgerichtet. Vom unteren Ende aus betrachtet bringt der Wasserfall Perspektive in den Garten. Die anderen Steine einschließlich des „Berges" etwas weiter hinter dem Flußbett sollen dem Garten Tiefe bringen. Die Arrangements wirken dynamisch, ganz gleich ob man sie von Grundstück aus oder von außerhalb betrachtet. Der Gesamteindruck des Gartens erinnert an ein Gemälde aus indischer Tinte mit Berggipfeln und einem gemütlich fließenden Gewässer.

Der Name des Gartens *Suirei-tei* bedeutet „Garten der grünen Berge", einem Satz des chinesischen Poeten Xie Huilian (397–433) „Ziehende Wolken erwecken die grünen Berge".

2. *Sanzon* Wasserfall.

Suirei-tei is one of several small municipal gardens in the town of Onishi created to showcase the locally quarried chlorite-schist stones. With a small tumulus behind it as an added attraction, the garden is built on a slant. The designer placed a short *sanzon* waterfall stone arrangement at the high end of the garden from which "flows" a dry streambed. A large, bold stone was put in the center of the garden, deliberately slanted opposite the direction of the stream. When viewed from downstream past the large stone, the low stature of the waterfall arrangement creates a sense of perspective. The other stone arrangements, including a distant-mountain stone in the rear downstream portion of the garden, were also designed to enhance the sense of depth. The arrangements are dynamic when viewed from either the front of the garden or from a downstream position.

The overall effect of the garden is that of an india ink painting of a range of mountain peaks along which a great river is leisurely flowing. The name of the garden, Suirei-tei, means "garden of green mountains," a phrase ("the fleeting clouds awaken the green mountains") from the Chinese poet Xie Huilian (397—433).

1. The stone arrangements are strong and unusual, creating the image of an india ink painting.
2. Sanzon waterfall stone arrangement.
3. Well-formed distant-mountain stone.
4. View of the garden from downstream, the large distant-mountain stone on the left.
5. Large, slanted stone in the center of the garden, providing it with movement and force.

⟨翠嶺庭⟩
Suirei-tei garden

4. Blick auf den Garten flußaufwärts mit großem Stein links.

3. Gutgeformtes Arrangement als Bergkette.

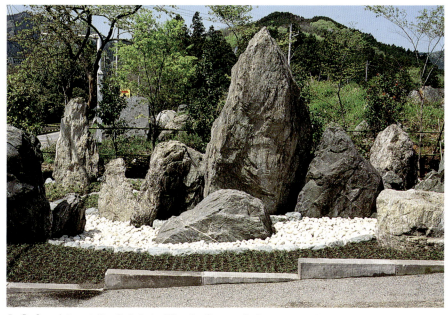

5. Großer schräggestellter Stein in der Mitte des Gartens gibt Bewegung und Kraft.

Design: Isao Yoshikawa. **Construction:** Onishi Garden Stone Business Cooperative; 1992. **Area:** 60 square meters. **Location:** Onishi, Gunma Pref.

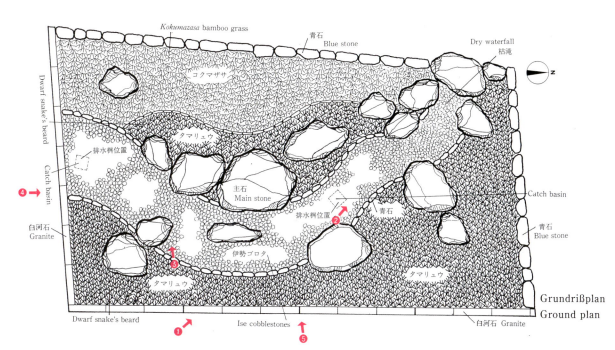

Grundrißplan
Ground plan

加藤邸庭園
The Kato Home Garden

1. Der Granitweg aus hellgrüner *Andesite* vom Gartentor aus überquert den Fluß und führt über den Rasen zum Haus.

2. Der Fluß ist von „Sourcing Rushes", „Sweet Flags" und schön angelegten Begrenzungssteinen gesäumt.

3. Der Wasserfall ist in einer natürlich gewachsenen Baumgruppe angelegt.

加藤邸庭園
The Kato home garden

4. Der Fluß, durch hohe Bäume betrachtet.

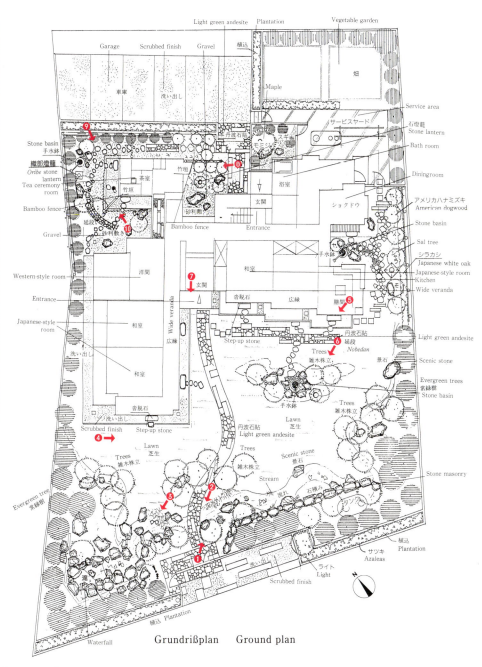

Grundrißplan Ground plan

Der Garten wurde gleichzeitig mit dem Haus erbaut, was das Einbringen von großen Steinen in den Garten wesentlich erleichterte. Auch die Gestaltung der einzelnen Elemente konnte an die einzelnen Zimmer angepaßt werden. Der Hauptpunkt war der Blick aus dem Wohnzimmer und dem Salon, der Rasen und zahlreiche hohe Bäume beinhaltet, die formelle Erscheinung des kleinen Innengartens vor dem Eingang des Hauses, die eine *Yunoki* Steinlaterne und einen *Katsura* Bambuszweigzaun beinhaltet sowie die Ansicht des Gartens bei Nacht.

Der Blick vom etwas abgesenkten Wohnzimmer ist besonders schön, einschließlich des gefliesten Weges, eines tiefer angelegten *Tsukubais* und verschiedenen Steinen und hohen Bäumen. Die Steine des *Tsukubai* wurden so angelegt, daß sich die Ansicht durch verschiedene Blickwinkel immer wieder verändert.

Ein Wasserfall in der südöstlichen Ecke des Gartens spendet dem Fluß Wasser, das unter dem zum Haus führenden Weg hindurchfließt. Der Fluß ist mit *Masonry* Steinen eingefaßt; die in die Umrandung eingesetzten Lichter reflektieren bei Nacht den gurgelnden Fluß. Der sich im gesamten Garten erstreckende Rasen läßt den Garten noch größer erscheinen.

Trotz der zahlreichen gepflanzten Bäume ist die Sicht nicht eingeschränkt. Folgende Bäume wurden verwendet: Walnuß, japanische Eichen, *Dogwoods, Sal* Bäume und *Storaxes*. immergrüne Bäume und *Ilexes* wurden entlang der Mauer gepflanzt und mit *Chinquapinien* und immergrünen Eichen kombiniert.

1. The granite and light green andesite path from the garden entrance crosses a stream and leads through a spacious front lawn to the house.
2. The garden stream is lined with scouring rushes, sweet flags, and well-arranged embankment stones.
3. The waterfall is in a natural setting of trees.
4. The garden stream seen through tall trees.

加藤邸庭園
The Kato home garden

5. Blick aus dem Wohnzimmer mit dem *Tsukubai* direkt davor, dem Rasen und einem Wasserfall ganz weit hinten.

7. Einige der großen Steine des gefliesten naturbelassenen Weges.

6. Der *Tsukubai* hat etwas Rustikales an sich. Durch den Fluß und den durch die Bäume sichtbaren Wasserfall erreicht der Garten Tiefe.

The laying out of the garden of the Kato home was done simultaneously with the construction of the house itself, allowing us to get large stones into the inner gardens easily and to arrange garden elements effectively in conjunction with the layout of the rooms in the house. The foci in the design of the garden were the view from the living room and parlor, which includes a broad lawn and numerous tall trees; the formal appearance of the small inner garden in front of the entrance to the house, which includes a *yunoki* stone lantern and a Katsura bamboo-branch fence; and the appearance of the garden at night.

The view from the recessed living room is especially pleasing, including (in order of distance from the house) a flagstone path, a recessed *tsukubai*, various scenic stones, and tall trees. The stones of the recessed *tsukubai* have been positioned so the appearance of the arrangement changes depending on the angle of view.

A waterfall in the southeast corner of the garden provides water to a garden stream that flows under the path leading from the garden gate to the house. The stream is lined with stone masonry; lights set into the banks reflect in the gurgling stream at night. The lawn extending from the bank of the stream toward the house is made to look more expansive by numerous deciduous trees spaced so as to afford an unobstructed view. These include maples, Japanese oaks, dogwoods, sal trees, and storaxes. Evergreens placed along the garden wall include ilexes, chinquapins, and evergreen oaks.

加藤邸庭園
The Kato home garden

8. Der sauber eingerichtete Innengarten hat einen Bambuszaun und eine *Yunoki* Steinlaterne.

10. Hinter diesem *Koetsu* Zaun ist ein *Shihobutsu* Steinbecken.

9. Der weiße Sand und die Bäume (Walnuß und *Ilex*) geben diesem Teil des Gartens eine saubere Erscheinung.

5. View from the living room, with the recessed *tsukubai* directly in front, a sprawling lawn, and the waterfall in the distance.
6. The recessed *tsukubai* has a somewhat rustic appearance. With the stream and waterfall visible through the trees, the effect is one of depth.
7. Some of the large stones of the flagstone path were left in their natural shape at the path's edge.
8. The cleanly arranged small inner garden includes a bamboo fence and a *yunoki* stone lantern.
9. The white sand and trees (including maples and ilexes) give this area of the garden a clean look.
10. Beyond this Koetsu fence is a *shihobutsu* stone basin.

Design: Kazuo Mitsuhashi. **Architects:** Nanri Architectural Design Office. **Construction:** Mitsuhashi Garden Design Co., Ltd.; 1992. **Area:** 972 square meters. **Location:** Ichihara, Chiba Pref.

黒澤邸庭園
The Kurosawa Home Garden

1. Der linke Teil des Gartens mit gefliestem Weg aus rotem Granit. Gegenüber dem Eingang ist ein tief angelegter *Tsukubai*, umrundet von Zwergzypressen.

2. Der Fußweg ist aus rostfarbenem Mischbeton mit großen eingefügten hellgrünen Platten. Unter den Zwergzypressen ist ein Steinbecken gebaut worden.

3. Der *Tsukubai* und die anderen Elemente – wie z.B. Steinweg, Steintreppen, Tropfrinne und Verwachsung – bilden eine einheitliche Senke.

黒澤邸庭園
The Kurosawa home garden

Das *Kurosawa Home* und das dazugehörige Umfeld sind höher als die Straße. Um diese Anhöhe zu befestigen, wurden Sandsteinklötze verwendet. Zwischen diesen Sandsteinmauern und der Gartenmauer sind Azaleen als sanfter Ausgleich gepflanzt worden. Die rechte Mauer ist weiter ins Grundstück gezogen als die linke Mauer; das schafft eine gewisse Asymmetrie und weckt zusätzlich Interesse. Im Garten rechts neben dem Eingang (direkt vor dem Salon) wurde eine Gruppe Zwergzypressen zwischen einem tiefer gezogenen *Tsukubai* Stein gepflanzt. Die Bodenbepflanzung ist *Kerria*, das eine gewisse Tiefe in diesem kleinen „Hain" erzeugt. Die gegenüberliegende Seite des Gartens ist mit ganz anderen Elementen, wie z.B. Rasen, Steinweg, einer Tropfrinne und einem gefliesten Weg neben der Rinne, angelegt. Der Fußweg ist aus rotem geschnittenem Granit mit Einsätzen in Karo-Form; bei Regen haben diese Steine eine besonders lebendige Farbe. Die Tropfrinne besteht aus kleinen Granitstücken mit abgeschrägten Ecken. Ein *Kenninji* Zaun, mit Walnußbäumen gesäumt, erstreckt sich vom Eingang des Hauses zum Badezimmer. Im südöstlichen Teil befindet sich ein Gemüsegarten, der durch immergrüne Eichen gegen Stürme geschützt ist.

4. Die schmale Seite des Gartens vom Hauseingang betrachtet. Die Größe des Gartens wird durch hohe Bäume noch unterstrichen.

1. The left portion of the garden, with its flagstone path of red granite. On the opposite side of the entrance path is a recessed *tsukubai* surrounded by dwarf cypresses.
2. The approach pathway is a rust-colored-gravel scrubbed finish with large pieces of light green andesite scattered in it. A stone basin has been placed among dwarf cypresses.
3. The recessed *tsukubai* and the other elements here—step-up stone, stepping stones, eavesdrop gutter, and undergrowth—form a unified whole.
4. The small side of the garden viewed from the house entrance. The size of the garden is offset by the use of tall trees.

Design: Kazuo Mitsuhashi. **Architects:** Kikuchi Design, Ltd. **Construction:** Mitsuhashi Garden Design Co., Ltd.; 1993. **Area:** 260 square meters. **Location:** Yachiyo, Chiba Pref.

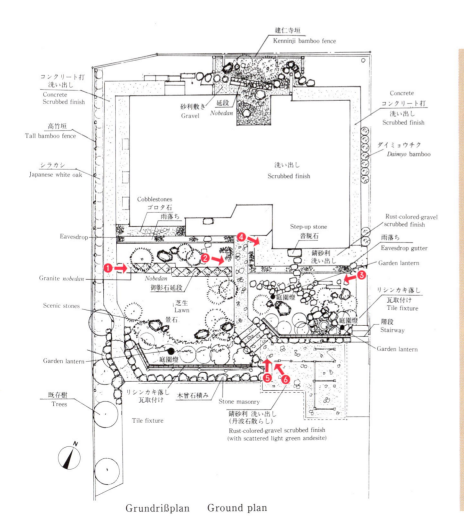

Grundrißplan   Ground plan

Stützmauern

Stützmauern, wie die aus Sandstein, die rund um den *Kurosawa* Garten gezogen wurden, können in verschiedenen Formen vorkommen. Das Wichtigste dabei ist, daß sie nicht die Schönheit des Gartens zerstören. Ein Gefühl für Technik muß vorhanden sein, um den Ausgleich zwischen kleinen, mittleren und großen Steinen zu schaffen. Wenn eine gute Basis aus Steinen geschaffen wurde, und nicht zu viele große Stücke aneinandergereiht wurden, sieht die Mauer nicht nur schön aus, sie hält auch sehr gut. Ein sehr gut ausgebildeter Konstrukteur wird nicht nur darauf achten, daß die Mauer stabil ist, sondern auch seinen eigenen Stil mit einbauen (Mitsuhashi).

Reinforcing Walls

Reinforcing walls, such as the one constructed of sandstone around the Kurosawa garden, can take various forms; the important thing is that they be pleasing to the eye. The mason must have the technical sense necessary to achieve balance among small-, medium-, and large-sized stones. Getting the basics right—such as placing the large stones correctly and not putting too many stones of the same size together—will result in a tolerably good appearance, but a truly skilled stonemason will be able to move beyond the basics and add touches of individuality to the wall. (Mitsuhashi)

黒澤邸庭園
The Kurosawa home garden

5. Zwischen Befestigung und Gartenmauer gepflanzte Azaleen.
   Azaleas are planted between the stone embankment and the garden wall.

The Kurosawa home and its surrounding garden are higher than street level, so the higher ground has been shored up with pieces of sandstone. Between these and the garden wall, azaleas are planted, providing a soft balance to the rough stones. The wall to the right side of the garden entrance is set into the property more than the wall on the left side ; this asymmetry adds an element of interest to the garden layout.

In the portion of the garden to the right of the entrance (situated in front of a parlor) is a stand of dwarf cypresses among which a recessed *tsukubai* comprising stones in their natural state has been placed. The undergrowth in the area is kerria, which adds a sense of depth to this small "grove."

The opposite side of the garden has quite a different arrangement of elements, including a lawn, as well as stepping stones, an eavesdrop gutter, and a flagstone path near the eaves of the house. The path comprises cut red granite arranged in a diamond pattern ; the stones become especially vivid in color when rained upon. The eavesdrop gutter uses small granite flagstones with beveled corners, resulting in a light appearance. A Kenninji fence lined with maples extends from the house entrance to the bathroom. The southeastern portion of the property is a vegetable garden ; this is lined with tall evergreen oaks as protection against windstorms.

6. Das halbmondförmige Fenster in der Gartenmauer ist ein interessantes Element.
   The half-moon window in the garden wall adds an element of interest. From inside the house, a lamp on the outside of the wall is visible through this window.

酒井邸庭園
The Sakai Home Garden

1. Der Eingangsweg (vom Haus aus betrachtet) ist aus hellgrünen Fliesen angelegt. Rechts ist eine Sandsteinbefestigung, und links ziert ein Bambuszaun die Garage. Ein paar wenige, aber gut verteilte Bäume mit Schotterabgrenzung lassen alles größer erscheinen.

Das Hauptproblem bei der Planung dieses Gartens war, die beiden Garagen mit den anderen Gebäuden und der Landschaft in Einklang zu bringen. Das Grundstück ist in verschiedenen Ebenen angelegt. Wir entschlossen uns also, die Garage und das Eingangstor im traditionellen japanischen Stil zu erbauen, was sehr gut zu dem Haus paßt. Da die Rückwand der Garage aus mehreren Zimmern des Hauses zu sehen ist, wurde sie mit lamellenförmig gespaltetem Bambus verkleidet; das Ergebnis sieht dem *Katsura* Bambuszweigzaun sehr ähnlich. Dieser Zaun hat zwei Funktionen – er verkleidet nicht nur die Garagenwand, sondern bringt auch die nötige Tiefe in die Fläche zwischen Haus und Garage. Egal ob die verschiedenen Ebenen des Gartens nun von Natur aus gegeben sind, oder extra aufgeschüttet wurden, in jedem Fall wird durch flach angelegte Bepflanzung optische Weite erzielt. Die hügeligen Flächen sind mit Gras, *Kumazasa* Bambusgras, Bäumen und *Cryptomeria* Büschen (im Hintergrund zu sehen) bepflanzt. Wir benutzten Sandsteinblöcke, um die erhabenen Flächen abzustützen. In einem Teil des Gartens wurde diese Begrenzung etwas tiefer in den Boden eingelassen und dient jetzt als Grundbefestigung für ein Steinbecken.

Der Weg zum Eingang ist durch den Lamellenzaun zu sehen. Auf halbem Weg befindet sich eine Lampe als zusätzlicher Blickfang. Wir pflanzten ein paar weitverzweigte Walnußbäume neben dem Weg, um einen gewissen Raum zu schaffen; wenn die Bodenbepflanzung zu wachsen beginnt, wirkt das Gebiet leicht abgegrenzt.

The main problems to solve in designing the garden of the Sakai home were harmonizing the two-car garage with the other buildings and landscaping, and working with variations in land level on the property. We decided to construct the garage, as well as the main entrance gate, in a traditional Japanese style that went well with the house. Even so, the rear wall of the garage was directly visible from several rooms in the house. We hid the wall with a fence of latticed split bamboo; the result is similar to a Katsura bamboo-branch fence. More than merely covering the wall, the latticed bamboo also adds an element of depth to the area between the house and the garage.

Variations in the topography of the garden, either natural or made by digging and piling up earth, are an effective means of making a small plot of ground look more expansive. We covered the "hilly" areas with grass, *kumazasa* bamboo grass, and trees, and planted stands of cryptomerias in the distance. We used pieces of sandstone to shore up higher areas of land. In one part of the garden, the embankment thus made was set deeply in the ground, serving as a backdrop to a stone basin.

The entrance pathway is visible from the outside through a latticed door. Halfway down the path is a lamp that adds an element of interest. We planted a few widely separated maple trees near the path to add a sense of space; when the ground plants eventually grow, the area will look less barren.

酒井邸庭園
The Sakai home garden

2. Verschiedene Elemente zusammen ergeben einen großen Platz und verstecken gleichzeitig die Garage links. Bambuszaun und Schotter vor der Garage sowie Bäume und Moos schaffen verschiedene Ebenen.

3. Die Pinien im öffentlichen Garten hinter dem Grundstück unterstreichen den Charakter des Gartens.

1. The entrance pathway (viewed from the house) is of light green andesite. To the right is an embankment of sandstone, and to the left is a bamboo fence covering the garage. The small number of trees and the gravel borders help make the area look more spacious.
2. Several elements work together to create a sense of space and hide the fact that there is a garage at the left: the bamboo fence and stones in front of it, the difference in levels, and the use of moss and trees.
3. The pines in the public garden beyond the property enhance the view of the garden itself.
4. The lattice door at the gate and the small lamp beyond it.

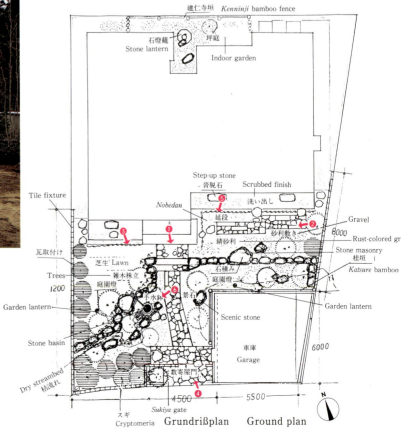

酒井邸庭園
The Sakai home garden

4. Eine Lamellentür als Eingang mit einer kleinen Lampe dahinter.

5. Laubbäume im Garten ganz im Gegensatz zur öffentlichen Anlage im Hintergrund.

6. Die Kombination aus Sandsteinbefestigung und Bäumen hat die Anmutung eines Gebirges.

5. The deciduous trees in the garden set off the pines of the public park in the distance.
6. This recessed part of the embankment and the cryptomeria planted around it look like something in the mountains.

Design : Kazuo Mitsuhashi. **Architects :** Kikuchi Design, Ltd. **Construction :** Mitsuhashi Garden Design Co., Ltd. ; 1991. **Area :** 125 square meters. **Location :** Nagareyama, Chiba Pref.

Gartenplanung

Wenn Sie planen, einen Garten anzulegen, nehmen Sie sich einen Moment Zeit, stellen sich auf Ihr Grundstück und überlegen sich ein Layout, das zum Haus, zum Umfeld usw. paßt. Wiederholen Sie das mehrmals während des Layout-Entwurfes, da sich Veränderungen ergeben können. Bevor Sie einen Designer beauftragen, sollte schon ein gewisses Grundkonzept des Eigentümers vorliegen. Der Eigentümer sollte mit dem Designer zusammen den Entwurf durchgehen, um Mißverständnisse zu vermeiden (Mitsuhashi).

When Planning a Garden . . .

When planning a garden, take a moment to stand at the site and get an idea of the lay of the land and the appearance of surrounding scenery, houses, and so forth. Do this periodically throughout the layout process, as surrounding conditions may change. Before hiring a designer, the owner should develop an image of how he or she wants the garden to look and how it should be laid out to be convenient. The owner needs to work with the designer throughout the design and layout processes to avoid misunderstandings. (Mitsuhashi)

小倉邸庭園
The Ogura Home Garden

1. Das Steinbecken entlang des Fußwegs zum Eingang ist ein interessantes Detail dieser Anlage.

2. Die langen, hohen Elemente sind gut ausgewogen.

3. Die Fliesen sind schön gelegt, die Platten gut angeordnet, und die Bodenbepflanzung schafft Harmonie.

4. Die Steintreppen zum Haus sind interessant angeordnet und von üppiger Bepflanzung umsäumt.

1. The stone basin along the entrance pathway adds an accent to approach area. The randomly arranged biotite granite stones and the coniferous trees enhance the atmosphere.
2. The long and tall elements of the garden are well balanced.
3. The flagstones are well arranged, and the stone masonry and ground cover harmonize well.
4. The stones in the steps to the house entrance are arranged in interesting ways. Much ground cover borders them.
5. The dry streambed (*left*) unites the areas of the garden on either side of the pathway. The evergreens along the fence enhance the background; a sense of distance is evoked when these are viewed through the spaces between the deciduous trees in the foreground.
6. The upstream portion of the dry streambed, made with cobblestones.

小倉邸庭園
The Ogura home garden

5. Das trockene Flußbett vereint die Abschnitte links und rechts neben dem Fußweg. Die immergrüne Bepflanzung entlang des Zauns unterstreicht den Hintergrund. Durch die Laubbäume im Vordergrund betrachtet, erreicht das Grundstück eine gewisse Weite.

6. Die aufwärtsfließende Bewegung des Flußes wurde mit Kieselsteinen so angelegt.

Zwei Hauptmerkmale des Gartendesigns sind Kaschieren und Eintauchen. Der Eingangsbereich des *Ogura* Grundstücks vom Gartentor zum Eingang erfüllt diese Merkmale. Die Mauer erstreckt sich von beiden Seiten des Weges und trennt den Garten von der Straße ab. Es gab jedoch schon ein paar *Cryptomeria* Bäume, bevor die Mauer angelegt wurde, die eine Einheit zwischen der Straße und dem Garten bilden. Der Eingangsbereich beinhaltet ein Steinbecken, *Cryptomeria, Sawara* Zypressen und *Masonry* Ziersteine, die als Befestigungssteine dienen. Die Abstände zwischen den Steinen sind groß genug, daß Pflanzen hindurchwachsen können.

Am Ende des Wegs sind ein paar Steinstufen. Von dort aus erhält man einen sehr schönen Überblick über den Garten. Der Garten ist relativ klein, und wenn sich der Weg geteilt hätte, würde der Garten noch viel kleiner erscheinen. Deshalb erbauten wir ein trockenes Flußbett, das unter dem Weg „hindurchfließt" und gleichzeitig die beiden Hälften miteinander verbindet. Die aufwärtsfließende Richtung wurde durch unterschiedlich große Steine erzielt. Der Rasen wächst unregelmäßig in das Flußbett und ist von einigen Bäume durchwachsen.

小倉邸庭園
The Ogura home garden

7. Der aufwärtsfließende trockene Fluß mit einer Tropfrinne links im Bild. Der Garten geht dann links weiter. Die Gesamtansicht des Gartens zu verhindern, ist auch eine Art von Design.

8. Zusätzliche *Cryptomeria* Bäume an beiden Seiten des Zauns vereinen die Landschaft. Es wäre zuviel gewesen, den Steinweg durch den ganzen Garten zu ziehen, deshalb endet er an der Veranda.

Trockenes Flußbett

Ein Teich oder Fluß verleiht dem Garten eine signifikante Schönheit. Leider sind Wasserelemente sehr schwer zu unterhalten. Eine andere Lösung ist z.B. ein trockenes Flußbett oder ein Teich, in dem man Stein-Arrangements anlegt. Das Flußbett kann sehr schnell zu einem echten werden, und das ist wiederum auch sehr interessant zu beobachten. Sorgfältig ausgewählte Pflanzen, die sich während der verschiedenen Jahreszeiten ändern, sind zusätzliche Elemente, die trockene Landschaften verschönern (Mitsuhashi).

Dry Streambeds

A pond or stream provides a garden with a significant element of beauty. Unfortunately, bodies of water on one's property are very difficult to maintain. The solution can often be found in the use of a dry streambed or pond, using arrangements of stones. The streambed may briefly become "real" during a rainstorm, but this itself adds an element of interest. Careful use of plants that change with the seasons will add further beauty to the dry streambed or pond. (Mitsuhashi)

Two principles of garden design are hiding and dividing. The approach area from the garden gate to the house on the Ogura property has elements exemplifying both of these. The wall extending from both sides of the approach area separates the inside of the garden from the outside. However, a pair of cryptomeria trees that were on the property before we laid out this garden straddles the wall, thus creating a sense of unity between the inside and outside. The approach area includes a stone basin, cryptomerias, sawara cypresses, and decorative stone masonry to shore up the ground. The joints between the stones are large enough to allow ground cover to grow in them.

At the end of the entrance pathway are some stairs, at the top of which the garden proper becomes visible. The garden is relatively small, and if we had allowed the pathway to divide it into two distinct parts, it would appear to be that much smaller. We thus used a dry streambed, crossing "under" the pathway, as a means of integrating the two sides of the garden into a single design. The upstream portion of the streambed uses rough, irregular stones to distinguish is from the downstream portion, which has large, rounded cobblestones. The garden lawn slopes gently down into the streambed and is planted with a few deciduous trees.

7. The upstream portion of the dry streambed, with an eavesdrop gutter visible on the left. The garden continues to the left. Preventing a complete view of the garden from any one point is one technique of design.
8. Planting extra cryptomeria trees on both sides of the fence helped unify the scenery. Laying stepping stones all the way to the inside of the garden would be too much, so they stop at the porch.
9. View from the house of the downstream portion of the dry streambed, with azaleas on its banks. Tall evergreens block off the outside completely.
10. Eavesdrop gutter (*foreground*) and flagstone path.
11. The garden space has a clean look overall.

小倉邸庭園
The Ogura home garden

9. Blick vom Haus auf den abwärts „fließenden" Fluß, gesäumt von Azaleen.

10. Tropfrinne (im Vordergrund) mit Fußweg aus Fliesen.

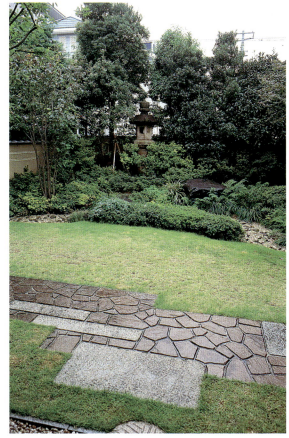

Design : Kazuo Mitsuhashi. **Architects :** Kikuchi Design, Ltd. **Construction :** Mitsuhashi Garden Design Co., Ltd. ; 1990. **Area :** 170 square meters. **Location :** Chiba, Chiba Pref.

11. Der Garten ist aus jedem Blickwinkel sehr übersichtlich.

T邸庭園
Home Garden in Kashima

1. Die Steinmauer im Hintergrund verleiht dem Garten Abgeschlossenheit. Das Steinbecken steht im Mittelpunkt zu den anderen Elementen im Garten, während das Moos auflockernd wirkt.

Dieses *Home* in *Kashima* (dessen Besitzer anonym bleiben möchte) befindet sich in einer wunderschönen Umgebung mit Bäumen des *Kashima Jingu* Schreines im Hintergrund. Die Bäume schaffen eine gewisse Tiefe. (Deshalb konnte sich der Designer nur auf den Garten konzentrieren.) Weil das Haus, das Gartentor und die Garage ziemlich geräumig sind, entschieden wir uns, den Garten in einer sehr entspannten Form anzulegen. Die Fläche rund um den Eingang wurde so angelegt, daß Besucher nur einen flüchtigen Blick auf den Garten werfen können. Erst wenn sie den Eingang erreicht haben, wird der Gesamtanblick auf den Garten frei. Um einen Gegensatz zu dem vielen Grün hinter dem Schrein zu erreichen, wurden Laubbäume (Walnußbäume und japanische Eichen) im Garten gepflanzt. Um weiterhin Abwechslung zu schaffen, erbauten wir eine niedrige Mauer aus Steinquadern entlang der großen Gartenmauer, die auf beiden Seiten in Erdwällen endet. Der Mittelpunkt des Gartens ist ein Steinbecken mit großen Steinen als Accessoires; Bäume und andere Steine wurde so plaziert, daß ihre Energie in Richtung Becken „strömt". Der Boden ist mit Moos ausgelegt, während verschiedene Farnarten natürlich auf diesem Untergrund wachsen und somit den Garten zieren. Ein Fußweg aus Fliesen wurde diagonal in größerem Abstand zum Haus ausgelegt und zieht mehr Aufmerksamkeit auf sich als ein gewöhnlicher Fußweg. Auf der gegenüberliegenden Seite des Eingangswegs befindet sich ein drei Meter großer Platz zwischen dem Haus und der Garage. Drei Grundelemente bestimmen diesen Platz: ein sehr feiner *Katsura* Bambuszaun verkleidet die Garage, Moos als Bodenbepflanzung und eine *Yunoki* Steinlaterne.

2. Die sich ausbreitende Mauer schafft eine gewisse Weitläufigkeit.

1. The stone wall in the background gives a sense of unity to the garden. The stone basin is the focal point for the other objects in the garden, while the moss adds a touch of softness.
2. The wall extending here helps provide a sense of spaciousness.
3. The approach area, with a Katsura bamboo-branch fence hiding the garage.
4. Another view of the Katsura bamboo-branch fence. The ground cover includes moss, ferns, and *sakaki*.
5. *Yunoki* stone lantern.

T邸庭園
Home garden in Kashima-machi

3. Der Zugang zum Haus mit einem *Katsura* Bambuszaun verkleidet die Garage.

4. Der *Katsura* Bambuszaun aus einem anderen Blickwinkel. Die Bodenbepflanzung besteht aus Moos, Farnen und *Sakaki*.

5. *Yunoki* Steinlaterne.

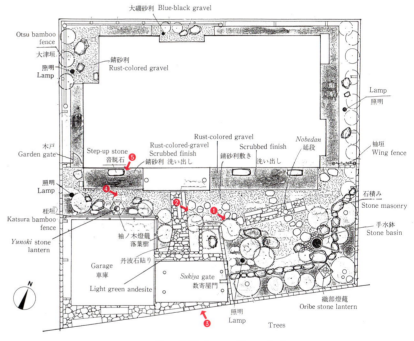

Grundrißplan   Ground plan

This home in Kashima (whose owner preferred to remain anonymous) is in a beautiful location, with the trees of Kashima Jingu shrine as a backdrop to provide a sense of depth (which allowed the designer to concentrate on the garden itself). Because the house, gate, and garage are all rather expansive, we decided to strive for a relaxed atmosphere in the layout of the garden. We set up the area around the approach from the gate to the house in a way that would allow visitors to catch glimpses of the main garden (to the right), but not to see it fully until they reach the entrance and look back.

To set off the mass of greenery on the shrine grounds beyond the main garden, we planted deciduous trees (including maples and Japanese oaks) in the garden. Further, to add variation, we made a low wall of stone masonry inside the main garden wall, tapering the ends of this into mounds of earth. The centerpiece of the main garden is a stone basin with large accessory stones; trees and other stones in the garden have been placed so that their "energy" seems to be moving toward this basin. The ground itself is covered with moss, while various ferns that grow naturally on the shrine grounds make up the undergrowth. A flagstone path laid out diagonally with respect to the house adds further interest, as does a path of stepping stones.

On the opposite side of the entrance pathway is a three-meter-deep space between the house and the garage. Three basic elements constitute this narrow space: a very fine Katsura bamboo-branch fence to hide the garage, moss on the ground, and a *yunoki* stone lantern.

Design: Kazuo Mitsuhashi. **Architects:** Kikuchi Design, Ltd. **Construction:** Mitsuhashi Garden Design Co., Ltd.; 1990. **Area:** 220 square meters. **Location:** Kashima, Ibaraki.

岸本邸庭園
The Kishimoto Home Garden

2. Aus dem richtigen Blickwinkel betrachtet, erhält man eine wunderschöne Gesamtansicht der Steinplatten.

3. Durch die Lampe scheint das Moos im Dunkeln zu leuchten. Die *Cyptomeria* und Walnußbäume erhalten eine leichte Maserung.

1. The tea ceremony garden is beyond the wicket, and the bath garden is beyond the Katsura bamboo-branch fence in the rear.
2. Getting the details of the stonework right results in an attractive overall appearance.
3. In the dark, the moss appears to float in the lamplight. The cryptomerias and maples provide a light texture.
4. The streambed and waterfall of the main garden. The garage is under this part of the garden. Cryptomerias and cypresses add a sense of depth.
5. The cobblestones harmonizes the streambed with its surroundings.
6. The *tsukubai* of the tea ceremony garden viewed through the entrance (larger than it would ordinarily be, to enhance the view) of the tea ceremony house.
7. The stones of the *tsukubai* are from old bridge pilings.

1. Der Teegarten ist hinter dem Gartentor, und der Badegarten befindet sich hinter dem *Katsura* Bambuszweigzaun im Hintergrund.

4. Das Flußbett und der Wasserfall des Hauptgartens. Die Garage befindet sich genau unter diesem Teil des Gartens. *Cryptomeria* und Zypressen erzielen die nötige Tiefe.

5. Die Kieselsteine vereinen das Flußbett mit seiner Umgebung.

岸本邸庭園
The Kishimoto home garden

6. Das *Tsukubai* des Teegartens durch den Eingang betrachtet (etwas vergrößert dargestellt).

Dieser Garten wurde in Zusammenarbeit mit Designer und Besitzer gestaltet. Besonders in diesem Fall wird deutlich, was eine Zusammenarbeit von zwei unterschiedlichen Betrachtungsweisen hervorzaubern kann. Die Fläche rund um das *Kishimoto Home* kann in verschiedene Abschnitte eingeteilt werden – Eingangsgebiet, Teegarten, Garten neben dem Badezimmer und Hauptgarten. Wir trennten den Garten vor dem Badezimmer durch eine Steinmauer, die mit einem *Katsura* Bambuszweigzaun besetzt ist. Das Eingangsgebiet ist ganz schlicht angelegt und verbindet den Hauseingang mit dem Teegarten. Der letztere ist zum Teil mit einem *Amida* Zaun (gewebter Bambuszaun) eingefaßt. Das *Tsukubai* des Teegartens wurde so plaziert, daß es vom schmalen Eingang des Teehauses aus betrachtet groß erscheint.

Das Kernstück des Hauptgartens ist ein Fluß, dessen Quelle ein kleiner Wasserfall ist. Der Fluß wurde so angelegt, daß von jedem Raum des Hauses aus verschiedene Klänge gurgelnden Wassers vernommen werden. Da der Hauptgarten relativ klein ist, wurde durch gepflanzte *Cryptomeria* und *Sawara* Zypressen die nötige Tiefe erzielt.

7. Die Steine des *Tsukubai* sind aus alten Brückenpfeilern.

This garden was a cooperative effort between the designer and the owner of the house, and in this case we have a good example of what such cooperation can accomplish when the two parties appreciate each other's viewpoints as well as we did in this case.

The land around the Kishimoto home can be divided into an approach area, a tea ceremony garden, a garden near the bath, and a main garden. We separated off the bath garden using a stone wall topped with a Katsura bamboo-branch fence. The approach area is laid out simply and connects the house entrance to the tea ceremony garden. The latter has an Amida fence (a fence of bamboo woven together) around part of it. The tea garden's *tsukubai* is was positioned to appear large when viewed from the small entrance of the tea ceremony house.

The centerpiece of the main garden is a stream whose source is a small waterfall. We laid the stream out so that there are variations in the sound of the gurgling water according to what room of the house a person is in. Because the main garden is relatively small, a sense of depth and shade was added by planting cryptomerias and sawara cypresses there.

Design: Kazuo Mitsuhashi. **Architects:** Kikuchi Design, Ltd. **Construction:** Mitsuhashi Garden Design Co., Ltd.; 1989. **Area:** 200 square meters. **Location:** Chiba, Chiba Pref.

長松寺庭園
Chosho-ji Temple Garden

1. Die Pinien und Walnußbäume neben der Haupthalle wurden erhalten und mit großzügig ausgelegten Steinen verschönert. Der *Ryoanji* Zaun schafft Gleichgewicht.

In dem für seine zahlreichen Tempel bekannten *Takanawa* Distrikt Tokios befindet sich der *Chosho-ji* Tempel, der „Pure Land" Buddhisten-Sekte. Dieser Tempel ist auch als Ruhe-Tempel des Confucian-Gelehrten *Ogyu Sorai* aus der *Edo* Periode bekannt. Unser Ziel war es, sehr viel der alten Tempelmauern wiederherzustellen. Im Gegensatz zu Gärten von Wohnhäusern müssen Tempelgärten so angelegt werden, daß sie die Prediger inspirieren. Im Laufe der Zeit sollte der Garten Gelassenheit erreichen.

Wir erweiterten den Steinweg vom Tor zum Tempel und bepflanzten ihn seitlich. Dies grenzt den Weg deutlich ab. Um die anderen Wege zu den Wohnräumen des Priesters und der Empfangshalle vom Hauptweg zu unterscheiden, sind diese mit hellgrünen Platten ausgelegt. Der Weg vom Parkplatz ist aus Waschbeton.

Wir benutzten die abgetragene Erde des Parkplatzes, um die Fläche neben der Haupthalle anzuheben. Hier wurde ein *Sanzon* Steinarrangement aus grob aussehenden, eckigen Chlorit-Schist-Steinen aufgestellt. Für die Gesamterscheinung dieses Grundstücks mußten wir die Blickwinkel vom Haupttor, von der Haupthalle und vom Parkplatz beachten. Wir ließen die schon vorhandenen Bäume – wie Walnuß, Kirsch, Pinien und *Podocarps* – stehen und veränderten Laternen, Steinbecken und Steine in ihre von uns vorgesehenen Stellungen. *Kokumazasa* Bambusgras und *Dwarf Snake's Beard* wachsen um die Steinarrangements. Ein *Ryoanji* Zaun im Hintergrund scheint das Steinarrangement am Boden zu überfluten. Im Layout für den Innengarten waren die Blickwinkel aus der Empfangshalle und den Wohnräumen zu beachten. Die schon vorhandenen *Camphor* Bäume und *Chinquapinien* sind groß, aber schon etwas dünn; deshalb wurden die Bäume stark beschnitten und die Rasenfläche zusätzlich erweitert. Wir plazierten ein Steinarrangement so, daß es sehr gut von der Empfangshalle aus zu sehen war. Die neben den Fenstern des Tempelgebäudes gepflanzten Walnußbäume verändern das Gesamtbild des Gartens mit den Jahreszeiten; die Bäume und zahlreichen Lampen auf dieser Fläche scheinen ein Buddhisten-Paradies darzustellen.

1. The pines and maples of the garden next to the main hall were retained, and a widely spaced stone arrangement was added. The Ryoanji fence provides balance.
2. The main stones of the same arrangements, with *kokumazasa* bamboo grass, dwarf snake's beard, and ferns.
3. The stones are chlorite-schist. Because of the small size of the arrangements, the stones are placed in a way that evokes a sense of energy.
4. A diorite stone basin, part of a stone arrangement.

本堂脇の庭
Side garden of the main hall

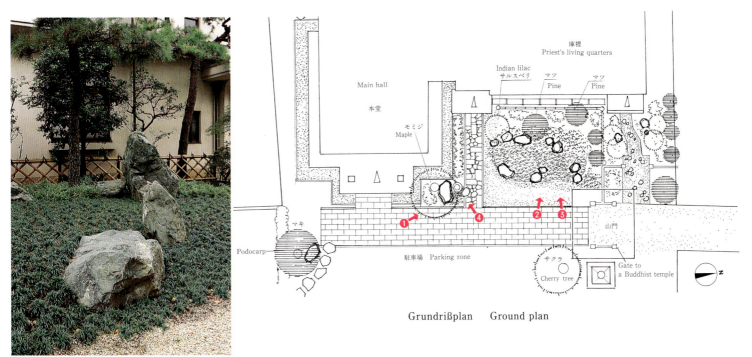

Grundrißplan Ground plan

2. Die Hauptsteine dieses Arrangements mit *Kokumazasa* Bambusgras, *Dwarf Snake's Beard* und Farnen.

3. Chlorit-Schist-Steine. Wegen der begrenzten Fläche des Arrangements wurden die Steine so ausgelegt, um Kraft und Energie auszustrahlen.

4. Ein *Diorit* Steinbecken ist Teil des Steinarrangements.

Steinarrangements

Das Hauptziel von Steinarrangements ist es, Raum zu schaffen, auch wenn die Steine selbst wieder Platz beanspruchen. Wie können Steinarrangements Raum schaffen? Einfach erklärt – man darf sich keine Gedanken um den Platz machen, denn sonst kommt man nicht weiter. Stelle die Steine zuerst dahin, wo sie stehen sollen, und kontrolliere
erst dann aus gewisser Entfernung. Entferne jetzt die überflüssigen Steine – so wird Raum geschaffen (Mitsuhashi).

Stone Arrangements

The essence of stone arrangements is the creation of space, even as the stones themselves take up space. How can space be created in stone arrangements? Stated simply, do not worry about spacing at the outset, or you will not get anywhere. Place the stones where you think they should be; then, step back and look at the tentative arrangement. Remove any stones that seem unnecessary. In this way you will have created space. (Mitsuhashi)

中庭
Inner garden

5. Steinarrangement im Innengarten mit *Camphor* Bäumen und *Chinquapinien* im Hintergrund.

6. Der Hauptteil des Arrangements. Daneben befinden sich Walnußbäume und japanische Eichen.

7. Sogar relativ klein aussehende Steine können dazu hergenommen werden, um ein groß aussehendes Arrangement zu gestalten.

Located in the Takanawa district of Tokyo, an area known for its numerous temples, Chosho-ji is a temple of the Pure Land sect of Buddhism and also happens to be the resting place of the mid-Edo Confucian scholar Ogyu Sorai. Our task was to revamp much of the temple grounds. In contrast to the garden around a home, a temple garden has to be laid out in a way that inspires prayer. As time passes, the garden should develop a sense of serenity.

We widened the stone-paved approach leading from the main gate to the temple itself and planted greenery along it, thus enhancing the dignity of this important part of the temple grounds. To distinguish them from the main approach, the paths to the reception room and priests' living quarters are of light green andesite and have scrubbed finishes. The path from the parking area is of concrete with a scrubbed finish.

We used soil dug up for the construction of the parking lot to raise the ground level of the garden next to the main hall of the temple. Here we placed a sanzon stone arrangement using rough-looking, angular chlorite-schist stones. For the overall appearance of this area we had to take into consideration the views from the main gate, the main hall, and the parking area. We left in place the existing trees—maples, cherries, pines, and podocarps—and moved lanterns, stone basins, and scenic stones into more appropriate positions. *Kokumazasa* bamboo grass and dwarf snake's beard form the ground cover around the stone arrangement. A Ryoanji fence in the background makes the stone arrangement appear to be floating on the ground.

中庭
Inner garden

5. Stone arrangement in the inner garden, with camphor trees and chinquapins in the background.
6. The main portion of the stone arrangement, with maples and Japanese oaks nearby.
7. Even relatively small stones can be used to make a large-looking arrangement. The stone on the right is facing away from the arrangement, creating a sense of energy.
8. Another view of the stone arrangement. Care was taken in spacing and in the creation of a sense of movement.

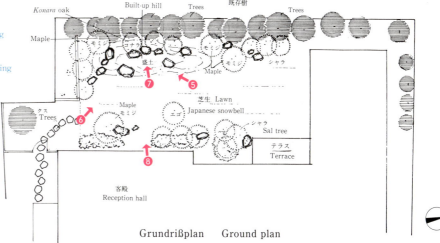

Grundrißplan Ground plan

8. Ein weiterer Blick auf das Arrangement. Es wurde sehr auf die Aufteilung und Bewegung im Garten geachtet.

The layout of the inner garden required that we take into account the views from the reception room and the living quarters. The camphor trees and chinquapins already here were large and overly shady, so we cut these back considerably, and also expanded the lawn. We positioned a stone arrangement in the garden so that it is pleasing to the eye when viewed from the reception room. Maples planted near the windows of the temple building result in a view of the arrangement that varies with the seasons; the trees and numerous lights placed in the area create the appearance of a Buddhist paradise.

Design: Kazuo Mitsuhashi. **Construction:** Mitsuhashi Garden Design Co., Ltd.; 1989. **Area:** Inner garden, 200 square meters; front garden, 110 square meters. **Location:** Minato-ku, Tokyo.

伊藤邸庭園
The Ito Home Garden

1. Blick vom vorderen Tor des Hauses. Das Haupttor befindet sich links davon. Der Eingangsweg dient als Befestigung gegenüber der sich links und rechts davon befindlichen Erde.

Das Hauptmerkmal des *Ito Home* Gartens ist, daß der Aufgang und der Garten zusammengehören. Da sich das Haus auf einer Anhöhe befindet, mußte über die Anordnung der Treppen von der Straße zum Haus nachgedacht werden. Eine Möglichkeit war, die Treppen direkt im Garten zu bauen: dies würde jedoch die Einheit zwischen dem Gartentor, der Gartenmauer und dem Weg zerstören. Deshalb entschied man sich für einen leicht ansteigenden Fußweg.

Der Weg ist aus Granit mit einer sanften Oberfläche, jedoch mit grob belassenen Vorderkanten. Die Treppen wurden unregelmäßig ausgelegt und laufen horizontal weiter in den Garten; diese Anordnung mit den Steinquadern ergibt den Anschein eines Gebirges. Ein Blickfang ist das Steinbecken am Weg, dessen Wasser die Umgebung wertvoller macht und ein Ruheelement im Garten darstellt. Außerdem zieht es Vögel an.

Bäume wie Walnuß, japanische Eiche, *Dogwoods, Kerrias* und *Andromedas,* sowie Bambusgras, *Spearflowers, Dwarf Snake's Beard* und *Pachysandra Sweet Flags* und *Scouring Rushes* befinden sich im Garten. Außerdem wurden immergrüne Eichen im Hintergrund gepflanzt. Bei Pflanzung verschiedener Bäume der gleichen Art muß ihre Höhe in Betracht gezogen werden. Zusätzlich sollte viel am Boden gepflanzt werden.

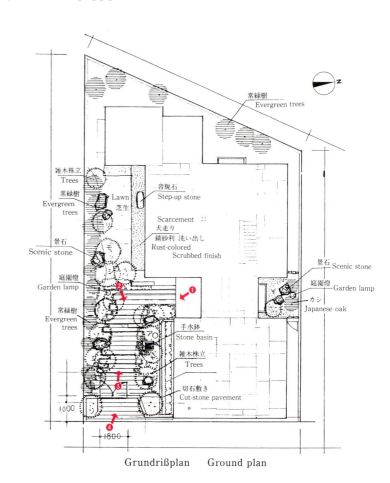

Grundrißplan　　Ground plan

伊藤邸庭園
The Ito home garden

4. Die Bäume außerhalb des Gartens bilden eine Einheit mit den Bäumen im Garten.

1. View from the front door of the house. The main gate is off to the left. The stones of the approach pathway also serve as shoring against the soil at the sides.
2. A stone basin provides a break in the long stairway, while the tall hedge in the background provides a screening effect.
3. To add interest to the approach pathway, the vertical edges of the steps were left rough and protruding steps were added.
4. The trees outside the gate provide a sense of unity with the garden inside.

2. Ein Steinbecken dient als Unterbrechung der langen Treppe, während die hohe Hecke im Hintergrund eine abschirmende Wirkung hat.

3. Als zusätzlicher Blickfang blieben die vertikalen Kanten naturbelassen. Außerdem stehen die Steine unregelmäßig über die Kanten hinaus.

The primary feature of the garden of the Ito home is that the approach area and the garden are one and the same. Because the house is on elevated land, a decision had to be made as to the arrangement of the stairs from the road to the house. One possibility was putting the stairs immediately inside the gate ; unfortunately, this arrangement often results in a lack of balance among the gate, garden wall, and the entrance pathway. We therefore opted for a gradually rising approach pathway.

The pathway is of granite, smooth on the surface but left rough on the vertical portion of the steps. The steps are placed at irregular intervals and have horizontal protrusions ; this arrangement and the presence of shrubs and ground cover evokes a sense of being in the mountains. A landing, or resting place, along the way contains a stone basin, whose water enhances the scenery, provides an element of calmness, and attracts birds to the area.

The trees and shrubs in the garden include maples, Japanese oaks, dogwoods, kerrias, and andromedas, while the ground is covered by bamboo grass, spearflowers, dwarf snake's beard, pachysandra, sweet flags, and scouring rushes. We also planted evergreen oaks in the background. The trick to planting a variety of trees is to plant two or three of the same kind near one another, taking into account their height. Additionally, much ground cover should be used.

Design : Kazuo Mitsuhashi. **Construction :** Mitsuhashi Garden Design Co., Ltd. ; 1993. **Area :** 90 square meters. **Location :** Chiba, Chiba Pref.

近藤邸庭園
The Kondo Home Garden

1. Das Wasser aus dem Steinbecken fließt unter dem Fußweg zum Eingang, dann entlang des Wegs und erneut unter dem Fußweg hindurch – ein Blickfang, wenn man auf dem Weg läuft.

Gleichzeitig mit dem Garten wurde auch das *Kondo Home* renoviert. Der Bau einer neuen Garage hat uns zusätzlich Erde für den Garten zur Verfügung gestellt.

Da der Weg zum Haus ziemlich lang ist, entschlossen wir uns, den Garten so anzulegen, daß die Elemente dem Besucher erst beim Entlanggehen auffallen. Das Haus z.B. ist nicht von jedem Teil des Wegs aus zu sehen. Die Bäume breiten sich aus (im beiliegenden Grundrißplan links unten) und sind so angelegt, daß der Eindruck entsteht, sie würden mit dem Hintergrund verschmelzen. Der Mittelteil dieses Eingangsbereichs befand sich in einer kleinen Senke; deshalb bildete sich bei Regen eine Pfütze. Diese Senke wurde dann mit Erde aufgefüllt, und das Wasser wird nun von hier aus in einen Fluß geleitet, der vom Steinbecken aus gespeist wird und den Fußweg zweimal unterquert. Die Steinbefestigung (Fliesen), die Kieselsteine im Flußbett und die Bodenbepflanzung ergeben einen interessanten Kontrast. Wir haben den langen Fußweg mit hellgrünen Fliesen und Granitplatten ausgelegt. Der Platz vor dem Haus wurde ebenfalls mit hellgrünen Fliesen verlegt.

Die Bäume entlang der Gartenmauer sind *Ilex*. Der Rasen wächst großflächig, was einen strahlenden wunderschönen Anblick ergibt, der auch abends, durch die Laternen am Weg, noch unterstützt wird.

The laying out of the garden of the Kondo home accompanied a revamping of the house itself. The construction of a new garage provided us with additional soil for use in the garden.

Since the approach pathway is rather long, we decided to lay out the garden so that its features would unfold to visitors as they proceed along the path. For example, the house is not visible from part of the path. The trees jutting out into the lawn (in the lower left part of the accompanying ground plan) are spaced so that, when they are seen from the path, a sense of peering into the distance is created.

The central portion of the approach area contained a depression in the soil that resulted in a puddle when it rained; rather than fill this in with earth, we laid out the ground so that the water would drain away into a stream that proceeds from a stone basin and follows the approach pathway, crossing under it twice. The embankment stonework (of andesite), the cobblestones in the stream, and the nearby ground cover combine to create an interesting effect. We paved the long approach pathway with light green andesite and pieces of granite, and used light green andesite for the flagstone path in front the house as well.

The trees along the garden wall are ilexes. The lawn is spacious, resulting in a bright, pleasant view, which improves even further in the evening as a result of a series of lanterns placed along the approach pathway.

近藤邸庭園
The Kondo home garden

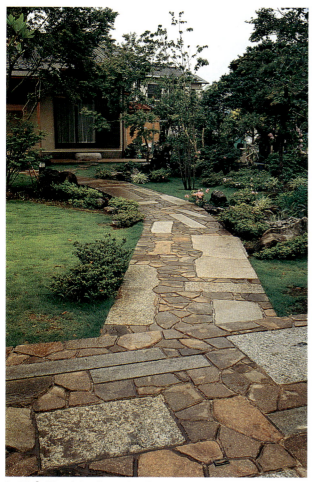

2. Dieser Weg wird auch von einer Kombination aus großen, dicken und kleinen, feinen Steinen eingesäumt.

3. Der Fußweg mit dem Eingang des Hauses.

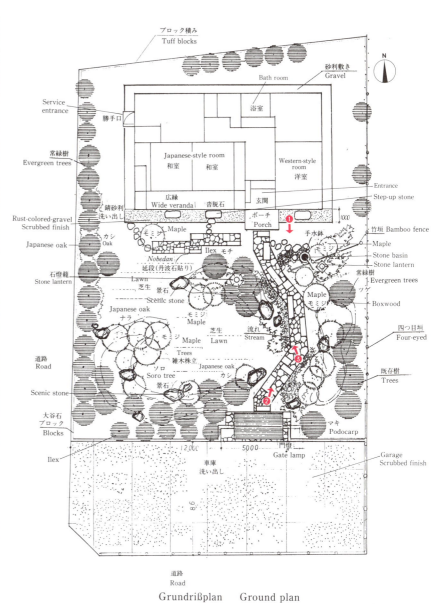

Grundrißplan   Ground plan

1. The water from the stone basin flows under the approach pathway, then flows along the pathway and back under it again—something to look at as one walks along the path.
2. The approach pathway contains a combination of large, bold stones and smaller, fine ones.
3. The approach pathway and entrance to the house.

Design: Kazuo Mitsuhashi. **Construction:** Mitsuhashi Garden Design Co., Ltd.; 1990. **Area:** 369 square meters. **Location:** Funabashi, Chiba Pref.

花島邸庭園
The Hanajima Home Garden

1. *Narihira* Bambus ist besonders für kleine Flächen geeignet. Der Fußweg ist aus Granit und hellgrünen Fliesen.

2. Diese praktische *Yunoki* Laterne verbindet die Elemente um das Eingangstor.

3. Die Stufe in der Traufe gleicht den Höhenunterschied des Grundstücks aus.

In den vorhergehenden, das Gartendesign betreffenden Diskussionen verdeutlichte der Besitzer, daß er von uns die Philosophie des *Furuta Oribe* wiedergegeben haben möchte. Dieser war ein Tee-Zeremonien-Meister und Künstler aus dem 16. Jahrhundert, den der Besitzer des *Hanajuma* Homes sehr schätzt. Solch ein Wunsch bereitete uns natürlich Schwierigkeiten; den Garten lediglich so zu gestalten, daß er schön anzusehen ist, würde den Wunsch des Besitzers nicht erfüllen. Außerdem stand nur eine sehr kleine Fläche zur Verfügung.

Was würde denn *Oribes* Kunst und Gedanken widerspiegeln? Wir beschlossen, daß es Darstellungskunst und wenig Zurückhaltung war. Um dies auszudrücken, benutzten wir große schwere Steinarrangements, die in einem kleinen Garten noch größer wirken. Darüber hinaus versuchten wir, Unerwartetes mit einzubauen: z.B. nur wenn Besucher das Haus erreichen und sich dann umdrehen, bemerken sie, daß einige der Steine des Fußwegs eigentlich auch Teile des Steinarrangements sind.

Da nicht viel Platz für Pflanzen ist, wurden Zwergzypressen verwendet, deren schmale hohe Form die dicken Steine noch größer erscheinen läßt. Auf dem Platz hinter der Garage wurde ein Teegarten angelegt. Um den Mangel an Platz auszugleichen, benutzten wir nur ausgesuchtes Material. Um sicherzugehen, daß der Bambuszaun künftig nicht sehr viel Wartung in Anspruch nehmen wird, wurden mit Bambus umwickelte Eisenpfähle als Stützen verwendet.

花島邸庭園
The Hanajima home garden

In the preliminary discussions regarding the design of the garden at the Hanajima home, the owner mentioned that he wanted us to reflect in our design the philosophy of Furuta Oribe, a sixteenth-century tea ceremony master and artist whom the owner held in high esteem. Such a request, of course, presented us with difficulties; merely making the garden convenient and pleasing would not fulfill the owner's desires. Additionally, there was only a small amount of land available for the garden.

What, then, would epitomize Oribe's art and thought? We determined that it was showiness, in a bold, not a coquettish, sense. To express this, we used large bold stone arrangements, which look that much larger in the small garden. Moreover, we attempted to create a sense of the unexpected: for example, only when visitors reach the house and look back do they realize that some of the stones that come up to the pathway are actually part of a stone arrangement.

Since there was not much room for plants, we put in dwarf cypresses, whose vertical lines make the garden stones appear larger. In the narrow space behind the garage we laid out a tea ceremony garden; to make up for the lack of space, we used very good materials. To ensure that the bamboo fence here would not require much maintenance in the future, we used iron posts, disguising them by wrapping thin bamboo around them.

1. *Narihira* bamboo is especially effective in cramped areas. Granite and light green andesite make up the approach pathway.
2. This handsome *yunoki* lantern unifies the elements of the area around the gate.
3. Steps under the eaves take care of differences in ground level.
4. This dynamic stone arrangement works well in the small main garden. Moving it as far from the house as possible adds an element of depth.
5. The relative heights of the fence and the tall stone of the stone arrangement makes the latter appear taller than it is.

Bamboo Fences

Bamboo fences are a bit of a luxury, given that they last only about five years. Durable plastic fences made to look like bamboo are now available, and some are quite well made. When shrubs are planted in front of them, no one really notices that they are plastic. They are appropriate for the gardens of restaurants and the like.

Another alternative is using steel bars for the framework and real bamboo for the frets. A framework of bamboo is difficult to replace when parts of it rot in the ground, but bamboo frets can be replaced relatively easily. The steel pieces can be hidden by wrapping them with thin strips of bamboo.
(Mitsuhashi)

4. Dieses dynamische Steinarrangement macht sich sehr gut in dem schmalen Hauptgarten. Es so weit wie möglich vom Haus wegzubauen, schafft Tiefe im Garten.

5. Die relative Höhe des Zauns und der große Stein des Arrangements läßt es größer erscheinen, als es ist.

花島邸庭園
The Hanajima home garden

6. Der wunderschöne Bambuszweigzaun ziert den kleinen Teegarten. Die Treppensteine sind aus hochwertigem *Diorit*.

7. Ein kleiner Garten birgt viele Schwierigkeiten für den Designer, jedoch ist ein sehr schönes Ergebnis möglich.

花島邸庭園
The Hanajima home garden

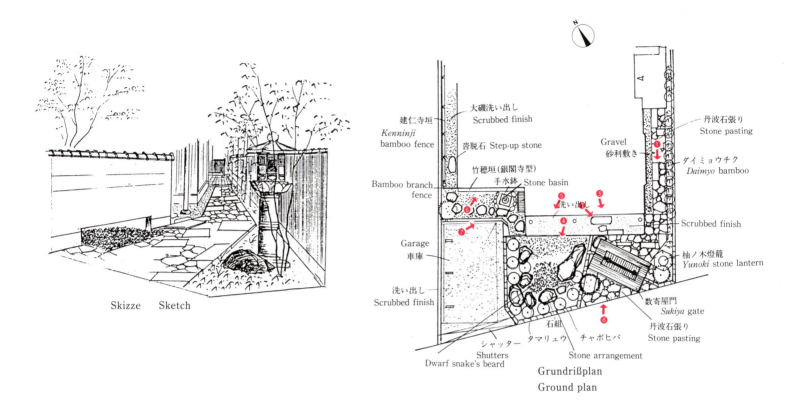

Skizze Sketch

Grundrißplan
Ground plan

8. Die lamellenartigen Fenster des Tors vermitteln Geschmack. Das Tor paßt sehr gut zu den Traufen des Hauses.

6. The beautiful bamboo branch fence unifies the small tea ceremony garden. The stepping stones are high-quality diorite.
7. A small garden presents numerous difficulties in design, but an effective result is possible.
8. The lathwork window of the gate adds a touch of class. The gate goes well with the lines of the eaves of the house.

Bambuszäune

Bambuszäune vermitteln einen gewissen Luxus, der mindestens fünf Jahre erhalten bleibt. Haltbare Plastikzäune, die wie Bambus aussehen, stehen zur Verfügung – einige davon sehen sogar echt aus. Wenn dann noch kleine Büsche davor- gepflanzt werden, ist kaum zu erkennen, daß sie aus Plastik sind. Sie sind sehr gut für Restaurantgärten o.ä. geeignet.

Eine andere Alternative ist es, Stahlträger als Stützen und echten Bambus für die Verkleidung zu verwenden. Die Träger sind sehr schwer zu ersetzen, wenn Teile davon im Boden verankert sind. Die Bambusverkleidung kann jedoch relativ einfach ausgetauscht werden. Die Stahlteile können mit schmalen Bambusstreifen verkleidet werden (Mitsuhashi).

Design: Kazuo Mitsuhashi. **Architects:** Kikuchi Design, Ltd. **Construction:** Mitsuhashi Garden Design Co., Ltd.; 1993. **Area:** 30 square meters. **Location:** Chiba, Chiba Pref.

天龍寺庭園
Tenryu-ji Temple Garden

1. Eine Gesamtansicht der *Horai* Formation, direkt vor dem Eingang der Haupthalle.
   A full view of the horai formation, which stands in front of the entrance to the main hall.

Tenryu-ji, bekannt als der erste von fünf *Kyoto* Tempeln, wurde 1339 auf dem Grund des *Kameyama* Palasts von *Takuni Ashikaga* zum Gedenken an Kaiser *Godaigo* gebaut, der in diesem Jahr in *Yoshino* unter unglücklichen Umständen verstarb.

Der Zen-Tempel würde *Arashiyama* als Rückhalt haben und beiden Trost spenden (dem toten Kaiser, der hier in jungen Jahren studierte und dem Geist aller Krieger, Feinde und allen, die in der Schlacht gestorben sind).

Der Tempelgarten ist im *Sogenchi* Stil eigens vom hohen Priester *Muso*, und in Gedenken an die idyllische Dynastie der *Yamato* Kultur nachempfunden. Außerdem befinden sich darin auch Zen-Gemälde im *Sung-Yuan* Stil. Es entstand ein Garten mit schlichter Schönheit und historischer Bedeutung.

Diese Fläche verlangt einen Garten mit großer Aussagekraft und deshalb wurde eine Felsenformation geplant. Im Gegensatz zu dem Garten im hinteren Teil mit dem rundlaufenden Teich sollte der Vorgarten im Zen-Stil die Insel der ewigen Jugend nachstellen. Der Effekt einer mit indischen Wasserfarben gefertigten Zeichnung im Zen-Stil wurde nachempfunden. Die Zeichen vor dem Garten sagen aus, daß es sich um einen *Horai* Garten handelt, und daß der Berg – laut einer chinesischen Legende – einer der drei weisen Berge sei, die über dem östlichen Meer stehen und von einem Einsiedler belebt werden, und dieser Berg das Land des ewigen Lebens sei. Die anderen Steine stellen *Shaka Sanson* (die drei Buddhas) dar, in der Mitte *Shaka Nyorai*, links *Fuken Bosatsu* und rechts *Monju Bosatsu*. Ein weiterer Stein repräsentiert *Rakan*, der Beschützer-Gott.

Egal ob man diese Formation als symbolisch für den Buddhismus betrachtet oder die Aussagekraft der Natur bewundert, wenn man z.B. den weißen Sand als Wolken betrachtet und die heiligen Felsen ragen hindurch, so fühlt man die große Weite, die durch diese relativ kleine Fläche eingefangen wird. Man beobachtet betende Menschen vor diesen Steinen, und es scheint, als ob die Steine sprechen würden.

Known as the first of Kyoto's Five Temples, Tenryu-ji was ordered to be built at the site of the Kameyama Palace by Takuji Ashikaga in 1339, in memory of the Emperor Godaigo, who had passed away that year in unfortunate circumstances in Yoshino. The Zen temple would have Arashiyama as a backdrop, and would offer consolation to both the dead emperor, who had studied on its grounds as a boy, and the spirits of all warriors, enemy and ally alike, who had died in battle.

The temple has a garden of the *sogenchi* style, reputedly built by the master priest Muso, which is intended as a depiction of the idyllic dynasty of the Yamato culture, as well as a Sung-Yuan-style Zen painting. Against the backdrop of Arashiyama and Kameyama this old-style go-round pond garden has a waterfall rock formation and other natural rocks settings, and the result is a work of rare beauty, and a garden designated as a special historical site.

With a garden of this distinction on its grounds, we put much thought into the design of the front garden. Above this area of rising stones are the main hall and the priest's living quarters, two very large buildings. The space required a garden with plenty of force, and so a garden of rock formations was planned, and rocks brought in. In contrast to the go-round pond garden in the rear, the front garden would be a Zen garden depicting the Island of Eternal Youth.

Stones used in the construction of the Island of Eternal Youth formation were chosen especially for their weight, expressiveness, and suitability for achieving the effect of an ink watercolor of the Zen style. The sign in front of the garden says it is the Garden of Horai, and goes on to explain that is the mountain which is mentioned in Chinese legend as one of the three divine mountains, which is situated over the eastern sea, and upon which lives a hermit, and that this mountain is a land of eternal life; and that the other stones represent the Shaka Sanson (three Buddhas), with the center being *shaka nyorai*, the left being *fuken bosatsu*, and the right being *monju bosatsu*. Another stone represents Rakan, the God of protection, it explains. Whether

前庭
Front garden

2. Blick auf die *Horai* Formation vom Eingang aus in Richtung der Wohnräume des Priesters. A view of the horai formation as seen from the side of the entrance toward the back of the priest's living quarters.

3. Der Mittelpunkt der Formation. The central stones of the formation.

4. Auf dem Boden liegende Steine vor der Formation. Diese dienen dazu, die gesamte Formation zu stabilisieren.

Stones laid over the ground in the foreground of the formation. These stones serve to stabilize the entire formation.

one looks at the formation as symbolic of Buddhism, or sees in it expressions of nature, i.e. taking the white sand as a representation of clouds, with the sacred mountain rising above it, one feels the great sense of space exuded by this relatively small area. One witnesses people worshipping before these stones and it seems as if the stones are speaking.

Design: Saburo Sone. **Construction:** Sone Landscape Architecture Co.; 1986. **Area:** 64 square meters. **Location:** Sakyo-ku, Kyoto, Kyoto Pref.

長岡禅塾庭園
Nagaoka Zen Juku Private School Garden

中庭 Inner garden

1. Gesamtansicht des Gartens – sie zeigt den in der Mooslandschaft gepflanzten Bambus, eine Steinlaterne und Steine.

2. Blick auf den Garten vom Korridor aus.

3. Der Garten von einem Zimmer aus betrachtet. Der weiße Sand hellt den Innenhof auf.

前庭
Front garden

Die Renovierung des Vorgartens der *Nagaoka Zen* Schule war dringend nötig, und man begann damit, den Boden zu preparieren, die überflüssigen Bäume zu beseitigen und Moos zu pflanzen.

Dieses Grundstück wurde immer schon sehr gut gepflegt, und durch die Umpflanzung von Bäumen entstand ein aufgeräumter Eindruck. Durch die quadratischen Granit-Steinplatten und weiches Moos wurde auch diese Fläche mit der Zen-Atmosphäre erfüllt.

Der Hauptgarten kann von allen umliegenden Gebäuden eingesehen werden und wurde deshalb so angelegt, daß er aus jedem Blickwinkel gleich aussieht. Weißer Sand bringt Licht in die umliegenden Räume. Andere Merkmale sind drei moosbewachsene Hügel und kleine Steine sowie in das Moos gepflanzter Bambus. Die Steine und die Steinlaterne setzen Akzente im Garten und sind gleichzeitig die Hauptmerkmale. Die Offenheit schafft außerdem ein Gefühl von Raum zwischen den einzelnen Gebäuden und läßt die Innenräume größer wirken.

Dieser Garten verändert sich nur wenig während der Jahreszeiten, doch diese unveränderte Schönheit ist erfüllt von Sicherheit und Regelmäßigkeit. Die beiden Hälften des Hauptgartens sind aus gleichen Materialien angelegt.

A request was received to renovate the front garden of the Nagaoka Zen School, and work began with preparation of the grounds, including the removal of unnecessary trees and the planting of moss.

The area has always been well kept, and along with rearrangement of trees, the landscaping attempted to retain the uncluttered feeling. The laying of square granite stepping stones and soft mosses helped to imbue even this broad area with a Zen atmosphere.

The central garden is in an area which can be viewed from any of the surrounding buildings, and the garden was designed to appear as if it were being seen from the front regardless of the viewpoint. In order to cast light into the surrounding rooms a white sand area was given the leading role, with attention in one direction being on three moss-covered mountains and the small scenic stones, and in the other on the existing bamboo and stone lantern, where an island was built and moss planted to increase the sense of space.

The stones and stone lantern give accent to the garden, and in a sense feel like the central elements. The openness of the garden also creates a feeling of greater distance between the buildings, and a sense of extra space to the interior rooms, as well.

This garden changes little through the year, but this is a changeless beauty, imbued with security and regularity. The two gardens of the central garden, which are separated by the corridor, nonetheless employ the same materials, and have a common simplicity of design and overall effect.

4. Auch in dem angeschlossenen Garten schafft der weiße Sand einen großen Kontrast.

5. Der Vorgarten von vorn entlang des Fußwegs zum hinteren Teil betrachtet. Die quadratischen Steinplatten betonen die Elemente im Garten.

1. A full view of the garden, showing the bamboo studded moss island, stone lantern and scenic rocks.
2. The garden as seen from the corridor.
3. The garden as seen from a room. The use of white sand helps to illuminate the interiors.
4. Though an enclosed garden, the use of white sand and moss creates a scene of high contrast.
5. The front of the garden, looking along the stepping stones toward the rear. The use of square stepping stones pulls the elements inward.

Design: Saburo Sone. **Construction:** Sone Landscape Architecture Co.; 1991. **Area:** 176 square meters. **Location:** Nagaokakyo, Kyoto Pref.

全性寺庭園
Zensho-ji Temple Garden

1. Gesamtansicht des Gartens. Der trockene Wasserfall und die Sandinsel schaffen Platz in diesem besonders offenen und hellen Garten.

Der Hauptgarten des *Zensho-ji* ist seitlich und hinter der Haupthalle und kann vom Eingang, vom Lehrzimmer und den Gästezimmern eingesehen werden. Im Hintergrund sind die benachbarten Tempel, eine Statue und die Berge zu erkennen.

Im Mittelteil wurde der *Mt. Fuji* und ein trockener Wasserfall (*Karesansui*) nachgebaut, indem man Kieselsteine für die obere Schicht des aus dem Wasserfall fließenden Wassers verwendete. Der Fluß umrundet die Kranich- und die Schildkröteninsel im Vordergrund. Die Hügel wurden mit Büschen besetzt, in diesem Fall mit Rhododendron, während die schon vorhandenen Bäume blieben.

Näher am Gebäude befinden sich Platten als Fußweg und eine *Nobedan,* die zum Wasserbecken führen. In diesem Garten kann man immer wieder neues entdecken. Der trockene Wasserfall zwischen der Schildkröten- und der Kranichinsel wird von einer *Mt. Shumisen* genannten Formation geziert, die diesen Zen-Garten komplettiert.

Zur Abrundung der Gesamtansicht eines Zen-Gartens wurden zusätzlich Büsche und kleine Bäume gepflanzt. Neue Untergrundsteine wurden unter die Felsenformationen des Wasserfalls, die Schildkröten- und Kranichinsel gesetzt, obwohl schon andere Steineelemente im Garten aufgestellt sind. Unter den existierenden Steinen des Gartens befinden sich z.B. kissenförmige Steine, weshalb es nötig war, die exakte Form und Aussagekraft der Steine herauszufinden, um sie genau in die Formationen mit einzubauen bzw. die Formationen so anzulegen, um die Form zu verdecken. Durch den weißen Sand wurden erst einige Teile des Gartens richtig hervorgehoben, die zu der Atmosphäre des Zen-Gartens beitragen.

Der schönste Effekt des Gartens wurde durch den Kontrast zwischen dem grünen Moos und dem weißen Sand erzielt, doch bei längerer Betrachtung kommen auch die Steinformationen voll zur Geltung. Im Frühling blühen die Azaleen, und im Herbst genießt man die Laubfärbung. Die Hauptpunkte wie Moos und weißer Sand bleiben unverändert und werden trotz der jahreszeitlichen Veränderung bewundert.

The main garden at Zensho-ji is to the side and rear of the main hall, and can be seen from the entrance, the study, and the guest quarters. The background includes the neighboring temple, a monument and the mountains, and the garden was constructed with this in mind to offer a scene which is both open and relaxed.

In the center area we placed a stone resembling Mt. Fuji, and built a dry waterfall (*karesansui*) using *Ise* cobblestones for the upper reaches of the waterfall's flowing water. The stream was brought forth to surround the crane and turtle islands in the foreground. The mountains were depicted with trimmed shrubbery, in this case rhododendrons, while existing trees and new stones and moss were left on the moss island.

Closer to the building there are stepping stones and a *nobedan*, which lead one towards the water basin. Overall, this garden is one designed to be seen more than used. The dry waterfall between the turtle and crane islands is topped with a formation depicting Mt. Shumisen, completing the effect of a Zen garden.

Existing trees were used in the project, and emphasis placed on the atmosphere of the period, with new shrubs and small trees planted for added detail. New foundation stones were placed under the rock formations of the waterfall, turtle and crane, but for these scenic pieces themselves rocks already in the garden were employed. Among the existing stones used in the building were such things as carved pillar stones, and here it was necessary to discover the expressive quality of the stone for correct placement in the formations, or to use the formations to cover the flaws. By raking the white sand one brings out a pattern, further contributing to the atmosphere of a Zen temple garden.

The most conspicuous effect of the garden is achieved through the contrast between the green moss and the white sand, but after some time watching the scene the rock formation begins to assert itself. In

主庭
Main garden

2. Blick von der Haupthalle auf die Schildkröten- und Kranichinsel, die schon etwas mit Moos bewachsen sind.

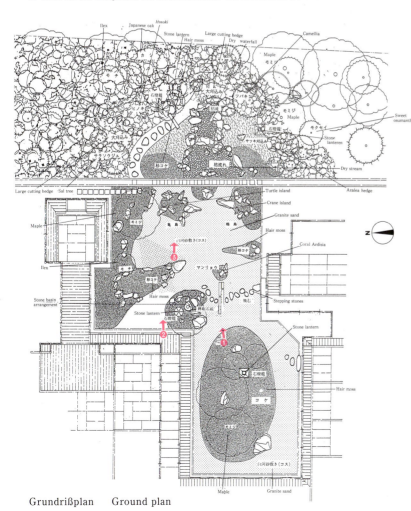

3. Im Hintergrund sind die Schildkröteninsel und der trockene Wasserfall sowie der *Mt. Fuji* Stein zu sehen.

springtime the azaleas blossom, and in the fall one can enjoy the seasonal colors. The central stage of moss and white sand remains unchanging, and must be observed through the changing seasons for its full effect.

1. A full view of the rear garden. The dry waterfall and sand beach create a following space in this particularly open and luminous garden.
2. A view of the turtle and crane rock formations as seen past the moss-covered peninsula from the main hall.
3. In the background are the turtle island and dry waterfall formations, as well as the Mt. Fuji stone. The water appears to flow down from the far mountains toward the foreground.

Grundrißplan   Ground plan

前庭
Front garden

4. Der Garten der Haupthalle. Die Pinien wurden in einer schlichten Landschaft belassen – typisch für die Enthaltsamkeit der Zen-Lehre.
The garden of the main hall. The pines were left in a simplified landscape of Zen austerity.

Durch das zweiflügelige Gartentor betritt man den Weg zum Tempel, der weiter zur Haupthalle führt. Diese offene Fläche wird für verschiedene Veranstaltungen genutzt. Auf Wunsch wurde in einer Ecke des Gartens unter schon vorhandenen Pinien eine Formation aus Kies und Felsen gebaut. In dieser Gegend fällt sehr viel Schnee, der sich, wenn er vom Dach rutscht, in den Tropfrinnen sammelt und bis zum Frühjahr nicht schmilzt. Unter den Bäumen wurde eine *Mt. Shumisen* Formation aufgebaut. Moos und Steine zieren die schneebedeckten Gebieten. Dieser Garten bringt das Wasser aus dem hinteren Teil nach vorn und fließt in weißem Sand aus. Die feine Oberfläche des Sands stellt die Reinheit des Tempels dar. Eine Ecke vor der Haupthalle wurde auch in diesem Stil angelegt – Sand und Steine rund um die Pinie – der Blick vom Tor in Richtung Halle ist somit ausgeglichen.

5. Azaleen und Zypressen als Kombination mit einer Steinformation, die *Mt. Shumisen* darstellt.
Azaleas and cypress combine with these stone formations to represent Mt. Shumisen.

Through the two-storied gate one enters the approach to the temple, which leads toward the main hall past the rear of the storehouse. This open area is used for various events. A wish was expressed to have a garden built in one corner under existing pines, with the addition of shrubbery and rocks for decoration.

In this area snows are heavy, and the snow which falls from the roof tends to pile up under the eaves, not melting until spring. In the area where less snow accumulates, around the existing pines, we built a Mt. Shumisen formation. We planted moss and laid scenic stones in the areas where snow accumulates, establishing it as the garden's foreground.

This garden brings the water forward from the rear garden to the white sand. The raked surface of the sand represents the purity of the temple. Having a corner of the area before the large main hall landscaped in this way, with shrubbery and stones laid out around the pines, the view from the gate towards the hall is transformed from one which is unendearing to one which is restful.

Design: Saburo Sone. **Construction:** Sone Landscape Architecture Co.; 1994. **Area:** 875 square meters. **Location:** Mineyama-cho, Naka-gun, Kyoto Pref.

真如堂庭園
Shinnyo-do Hall Garden

1. Gesamtansicht der *Nehan* Formation. Auf den mit Moos bewachsenen Hügeln ruhen Steine, die Buddha nachbilden.
A full view of the nehan formation. Upon the raised mound of moss rest the stones depicting Buddha.

Eine Steinformation, die den Buddha *Nehan* (Nirvana) darstellt, wurde östlich des Lehrzimmers gegen den Hintergrund der Hügel erbaut. Südlich von *Nyoigagoku* bis *Higashiyama*, dem Gebiet der berühmten *Tendai* Sekte, *Shinnyo-do* Halle, *Shinshogokuraku-ji* Tempel in *Kyoto*. Es wurde vom Tempel vorgeschlagen, daß der Garten von *Higashiyama* dem Ebenbild von *Nehan* Gebrauch machen soll. Deshalb entschied man sich, eine Steinformation als *Nehan* im Vordergrund zu errichten, und nutzt die Steine im Hintergrund als Kosmos. Um ein exaktes Bild zu schaffen, reisten wir nach Indien und China, um die heiligen Bilder zu studieren, und sammelten fünf Steine, um einen auf einem Kissen ruhenden Kopf nachzustellen. Auch andere Teile des Körpers wurden nachgebaut, um das Gesamtbild so natürlich wie möglich zu gestalten. Diese Formation stellt Buddha auf *Mt. Shumisen* dar, und die umliegenden Steine zeigen in Richtung *Shumi-Stand,* der traurige Ausdruck ist dem Buddha gewidmet. Zwischen den Steinen wurde Moos ausgelegt und vor der Formation Sand ausgebreitet, um das Bild *Nehans* weiter zu festigen. Eine Zypresse im Vordergrund mit einer Insel darunter soll in zurückliegende Zeiten versetzen. Es wertet den Garten auf, schafft Raum, Entfernung und Zeit zwischen dem Garten und uns. Um den aktuellen Stand zu erreichen, wurden Steine ausgesucht, die Buddha nachbilden und gleichzeitig genug Aussagekraft haben, um über den Steinen der Umrandung zu stehen. Der größte Teil der Steine wurde aus derselben Gegend genommen, um den gleichen Glanz, die gleiche Struktur, Kraft und Färbung zu erhalten. Das Ergebnis ist eine aussagekräftige Formation. Da man im Hintergrund Häuser unter dem *Higashiyama* erkennen kann, wurden Kamelien-Hecken, *Sakaki* und immergrüne Pflanzen gesetzt und angelegt, um die höheren Gebäude zu verdecken. In einer anderen Ecke des Gartens, neben dem Lehrzimmer, wurde ein Waschbecken aufgebaut und südlich davon eine im *Tomyou-ji* Stil gefertigte Steinlaterne aus der *Kamakura* Periode errichtet. Eine Steinformation mit Wasserbecken rundet das Gesamtbild ab.

A rock formation depicting the *nehan* (Nirvana) Buddha was built to the east of the study, against the backdrop of the hills running south from Nyoigagoku to Higashiyama, at the famous Tendai sect Shinnyo-do Hall, Shinshogokuraku-ji Temple, in Kyoto.

It was suggested by the temple that the garden should make use of Higashiyama as the image of *nehan*, but this was thought to be difficult, and it was instead decided to build a rock formation in the foreground to depict *nehan*, using the mountains in the background to express the idea of the cosmos. In order to create the image we traveled to India and China to study sacred images, then gathered five stones to create a head upon a pillow, and other parts of the body, trying as far as possible to make the resemblance clear. The image of Buddha was laid out on raised ground, and surrounded by mourners and animals, whose rock formations also serve to support the raised ground. The image is intended to represent Buddha upon Mt. Shumisen, and the surrounding stones face the Shumi-stand, their expressions of sadness turned toward Buddha's image.

Moss was laid between the stones, and sand spread to further strengthen the image of *nehan*. There is a cypress in the foreground, with an island beneath it, which is intended to transport one back to that distant age. And yet, the cypress is in the present, representing today, while the stone by the scene of nehan, which represents a priest in robes, tends to elevate it, as well as to create space, distance and time between it and ourselves.

For the actual preparation rocks were chosen which would serve to depict Buddha, and at the same time have the richness of expression necessary for the surrounding stones. Most of the stones were therefore taken from the same sources, with attention paid to their shine, texture, force and coloring. The result is unusually expressive stone formations. Since houses can be seen in the background, beneath Higashiyama, hedges of camellias, sakaki and evergreen were planted, and trimmed to blend with the foothills while concealing the high rise buildings.

In one corner of the garden, by the study, a wash basin was placed, and in the southern area a Kamakura period, Tomyou-ji style stone lantern, and a water basin stone formation, were added.

涅槃の庭
Garden of the Buddha's death

2. Der Vordergrund spiegelt die Gegenwart wider, und der hohe Felsen zeigt einen betenden Priester vor *Nehan*.

Wenn man einen Garten in Anlehnung an den *Nirvana* Buddha anlegen will, können verschiedene Probleme entstehen. Es ist jedoch sehr schön, einen Garten einem Buddha zu widmen, denn das trägt dazu bei, den Buddhismus besser zu verstehen. Hier wurde die schon vorhandene große Zypresse mit in den Garten eingebaut. Die Gegenwart, die Inseln und die Vergangenheit wurden symbolisch durch das ruhige Meer aus Sand vereint. Diese Art der Gartengestaltung sollte mehr gepflegt werden.

There are various problems in depicting an image of the Nirvana Buddha in the space of a garden, but it was a pleasure to create an image of Buddha which will help further the understanding of Buddhism. Here the existing large cypress tree was left standing, and the present world, the island, and the distant time of Buddha were linked symbolically by the crested sea of sand. Through the garden, and garden-building methods, the flow of time, and our long-held traditions, can be brought to life, and enter into the garden of the human heart. This is the kind of gardening culture we would hope to foster.

3. Die Zypressen stehen als Symbol der Gegenwart, der betende Priester wird durch den stehenden Felsen dargestellt.

涅槃の庭
Garden of the Buddha's death

4. Ein Wasserbecken, aus speziellen Steinen gefertigt.

5. Steinlaterne im *Tomyou-ji* Stil.

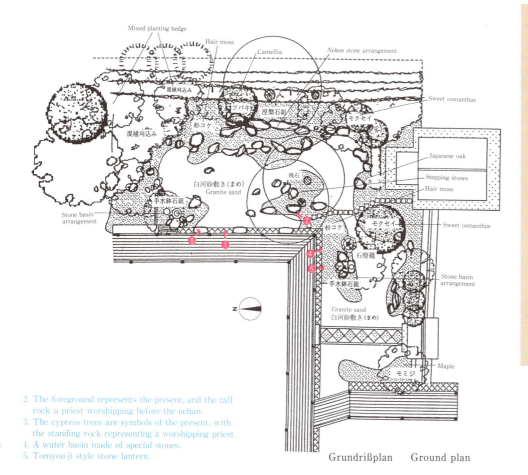

2. The foreground represents the present, and the tall rock a priest worshipping before the nehan.
3. The cypress trees are symbols of the present, with the standing rock representing a worshipping priest.
4. A water basin made of special stones.
5. Tomyou-ji style stone lantern.

Grundrißplan   Ground plan

Garden Themes

The Japanese garden is not merely a decoration for a building; in its shape and composition one should also see a spiritual beauty. And what is required for this, above all else, is an underlying theme. There are many types of themes, from light to heavy, and no two are exactly the same. One often sees lighter themes in the gardens of homes, while those of temples and sects often reflect more original insights.

However, and regardless of how original the concept of the garden may be, if the particularities of the landscape are not likewise beautiful, it will all be for nothing. And this is perhaps where the real difficulty of garden landscaping begins.

A theme is discovered in the first stages of garden planning, but even if the outcome is somewhat different in its realization, the ideal of the builder is to impress the viewers with the beauty of the garden. (Yoshikawa)

Design: Saburo Sone. **Construction:** Sone Landscape Architecture Co.; 1988. **Area:** 600 square meters. **Location:** Sakyo-ku, Kyoto Pref.

森邸庭園
The Mori Home Garden

1. Blick zum Eingang von der Straße aus.

1. On the road from the gate, looking toward the entrance.
2. The entrance garden, seen from the road above the gate. The feeling is open.
3. The chapel garden, with its central stone water basin.
4. The natural stone water basin of the chapel garden.

2. Der Eingangsgarten von der Straße aus betrachtet. Die Gefühle sind frei.

森邸庭園
The Mori home garden

3. Der Garten der Kapelle mit seinem Hauptstein und dem Steinbecken.

Dieser *Home* Garten ist auf einer erst kürzlich abgebrochenen Hügelspitze erbaut. Ein Privatweg führt von der Straße zur Vorderseite des Hauses und Gartens. Das Haus ist mit Büschen und Bäumen umgeben. Ein Originalstein des Hauses wurde in zwei Hälften geschnitten und gleicht jetzt die verschiedenen Ebenen der geschnittenen Granitstufen aus. Der Hauptbaum im Garten ist eine große japanische Schwarz-Pinie. Außerdem finden sich hier Zedern, Pinien und viele Walnußbäume. Das Eingangsgebiet ist mit einer Eichenhecke eingefaßt. Links neben dem Eingang befindet sich die Buddhisten-Kapelle *(Butsuma)*.

Dieser Garten wurde rund um einen vorhandenen roten Pflaumenbaum angelegt und enthält zusätzlich ein Wasserbecken, Steinstufen und ein *Nobedan*. Im Vordergrund steht ein Stein, der Gewicht in die Formation bringt. Vor der *Butsuma* ist Schotter ausgelegt, der zum Hauptelement führt. Zuerst wurde der Garten vor dem Eingang und an der *Butsuma* angelegt. Die gesamte Renovierung war in zwei Abschnitte eingeteilt. Als zweiter Teil wurde der Garten entlang des Salons wiederhergestellt. Er führt vom Eingang des Hauses zum Hauptgarten. Da dieser Teil des Gartens an die Terrasse anschließt, wurden sehr große Wegplatten verwendet, die das Hauptelement in diesem Abschnitt darstellen. Sie dienen außerdem dazu, den Blick zum Hauptgarten zu führen. Entlang dem Haus im Hauptgarten ist eine 1,8 m große Veranda. Unter der Tropfrinne wurden große, flache Steine verwendet. Wenn man dem Fußweg aus großen Steinen folgt, gelangt man in den westlichen Teil des Hauptgartens.

Die Fläche des Hauptgartens ist nah und tief. Rechts erblickt man einen Teich. Auf Wunsch des Besitzers wurden mehrere Kirschbäume im hinteren Teil gepflanzt. Deshalb hinten, weil sie so durch ihr Wachstum keine anderen Büsche im Garten verdecken können. Zwei Drittel der Fläche wurden für den trockenen Wasserfall verwendet, der mit Felsenformationen ausgeschmückt ist und dessen Wasserfall aus einer höheren Ebene fällt. Die dahinter verbleibende Fläche ist mit kräftigen Büschen bepflanzt, die Berge im Hintergrund symbolisieren.

4. Das Wasserbecken aus Natursteinen des Kapellen-Garten.

森邸庭園
The Mori home garden

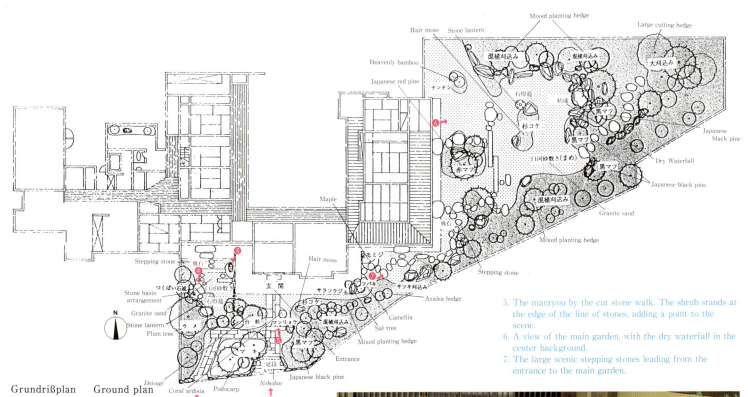

Grundrißplan Ground plan

5. The manryou by the cut stone walk. The shrub stands at the edge of the line of stones, adding a point to the scene.
6. A view of the main garden, with the dry waterfall in the center background.
7. The large scenic stepping stones leading from the entrance to the main garden.

Mehrere rote Pinien, Pflanzen und Blumen dienen als Vordergrund-Perspektive. Treppensteine und ein *Nobedan* umgeben die Moosinsel. Die Büsche rund um den Teich geben den richtigen Hintergrund, und die Pflanzen links schaffen eine Verbindung zu den Bergen im Hintergrund. Eine Insel aus Steinen und Moos sowie ein Strand mit einer kleinen Laterne breiten sich aus, um die Höhe der Formation zu verdeutlichen. Der Sandstrand ist aus *Shirakawa* Sand. Vom Haus aus blickt man auf den Teich und die Berge – man wird sich der Fläche, auf der der Garten angelegt wird, voll bewußt.

This home garden stands on a recently broken hilltop ground. A private drive leads from the street to the front of the house and the garden, which is surrounded by stands of trees. A flat stone from the original house was cut in two and used to divide the levels of the cut granite stone steps. The main tree in the garden is a large Chinese black pine, and there are likewise cedars and pines, and a mixture of maples. The area around the entrance is spaciously surrounded with a hedge of oak.

To the left of the entrance is the Buddhist chapel (*butsuma*) garden. This garden was built around an existing red plum, and included the addition of a water basin, stepping stones and a nobedan. A scenic stone was also placed in the foreground, adding weight to the setting, and gravel laid before the *butsuma*, lending definition to the central element.

The first project involved the garden in front of the entrance and the garden by the *butsuma*. The entire renovation was divided into two parts. The second project involved the garden extending along the parlor, which lead from the entrance of the home to the main garden. Because this section of the garden is connected with the terrace its stepping stones are large ones, and in effect are the main attraction of this section of garden. They also serve to leads the eye toward the main garden. Along the house by the main garden is a 1.8 meter wide verandah, and below its eaves large flat stones were placed. Following the stepping stones to the west side one arrives at the main garden.

5. Der Manryou neben dem Fußweg aus geschnittenen Steinen. Der Schotter an den Kanten weckt zusätzliches Interesse.

The area of the main garden is narrow and deep, with the area to the right affording a view of the pond. At the owner's request several dropping cherries were planted at the rear, in such a way that their growth will have no deleterious effect on the other shrubs in the garden. Two thirds of the area set aside for the dry waterfall is occupied by rock formations and the raised area of the waterfall, with the remaining area behind saved for cropped bushes, which represent the mountains in the background. In front of the building several red pines, and plants and flowers, were planted as foreground perspective, with stepping stones and a *nobedan* surrounding the moss island.

The stepping stones are also matched to the space of the garden, with slightly larger stones being chosen. There are trimmed bushes around the pond viewing area in the right background, and the plants on the left side are trimmed to achieve a continuity with the mountains in the background. In the middle area lies an island of stones and moss, while a beach with a low lantern lies before the dry waterfall, emphasizing the formation's height. The sand beach is composed of shirakawa sand. The stepping stones do not reach to the formation, but leave an open area before it. Here, when the cherries blossom, guests may lay down a covering and enjoy the flowers. From the house, the view of the pond and mountains is continuous, taking full advantage of the high ground upon which the garden stands.

Design: Saburo Sone. **Construction:** Sone Landscape Architecture Co.; 1987. **Area:** 780 square meters. **Location:** Mineyama-cho, Naka-gun, Kyoto Pref.

森邸庭園
The Mori home garden

6. Blick auf den Hauptgarten mit dem trockenen Wasserfall in der Mitte im Hintergrund.

Dieses Projekt wurde in drei Stufen und mehrere Jahre eingeteilt. Das Layout wurde zusammen mit dem Besitzer erstellt. Der Besitzer beschaffte das Material, aus dem ausgesuchte Steine auf den dafür vorgesehenen Flächen plaziert wurden. Seit Kirschbäume hinter die Formation gepflanzt wurden, ist der Garten wunderschön und einfach zu pflegen.

Die Bäume im Garten stehen als Kontrast zu den umliegenden Wäldern, und deshalb wurde nach Bäumen gesucht, die ein natürliches Bild ergeben. Die Wildblumen, wie die Büsche im Eingangsbereich, wurden ausgewählt, um Akzente im Gesamtbild zu setzen. Die Büsche neben der Kapelle sind für den Garten sehr wichtig.

In den verschiedenen Jahreszeiten wird der Garten in sich verwachsen und dann schließlich seine volle Schönheit entwickeln. Wichtig ist, daß der Garten nach dem Plan des Designers gewartet wird, um nach Jahren seine Vollständigkeit zu erreichen.

This project was undertaken in three stages over several years. The blueprints for the construction were drawn up with the participation of the owner, so that a final, unified plan for the entire project could be completed. The owner also supplied the materials, from which selected stones were placed at the specified points. The area of the garden is large, but with the planting of cherries behind the formation, it is at once beautiful and easy to manage.

The trees in this garden stand in relief to the surrounding woods, and an effort was therefore made to select trees that maintained a natural appearance. The wildflowers, like the shrubbery in the garden by the entrance, were chosen for the accent they lent to the scene. Those closest to the Buddhist chapel are the most important in the garden.

With the passing of the seasons the garden will grow into itself and attain its full beauty. It is important that the garden be maintained according to the scheme of the planner, and in truth it is the dedication to this purpose over many years that ultimately results in true garden-building.

7. Die großen Steine als Fußweg führen vom Eingang zum Hauptgarten.

熊谷邸庭園
The Kumagai Home Garden

1. Blick von *Salno* aus auf den Garten. Die große Sandfläche läßt den Garten größer erscheinen.
The view of the garden from the parlor. The large area of sand makes the garden appear broader.

Herr Kumagai ist Textil-Designer, der sowohl in Japan als auch in Übersee tätig ist. Sein Garten wurde ursprünglich für Gartenparties verwendet, doch nach der Renovierung seines Hauses wünschte er sich einen japanischen Garten, der zu verschiedenen Zwecken dienen sollte einschließlich des Meditationsraums.

Der Garten wurde in drei runde Flächen eingeteilt, zwei aus weißem Sand, die dritte als Wasserbecken. Der Kreis drückt Unendlichkeit aus, während die Wellen im Wasser und die Rillen im Sand Ausbreitung symbolisieren.

Das Wasserbecken ist aus *Shigaraki* Töpferarbeit und kann beliebig umgestellt werden. Ein Kreis ist einfacher anzulegen als ein Viereck und bietet sich als Sammelplatz an. Das Wasserbecken ist gleichzeitig ein *Tsukubai* und sammelt das Wasser für den Tee. Die Bewegung der Wasseroberfläche kann von den Steintreppen oder dem *Nobedan,* der über den Sand führt, aus beobachtet werden. Der Garten kann sowohl vom alten Haus, vom Hausanbau als auch von den Gartenstühlen eingesehen werden.

Der Garten ist von Büschen und Bäumen umgeben und wirkt trotzdem offen, da die Pflanzen entlang der Mauer und im Garten sehr gut angelegt wurden. Der zwischen dem Haus und dem Anbau verlaufende Weg aus geschnittenen Steinplatten wurde durch Natursteine ersetzt, um einen abgerundeten Effekt zu erzielen. Dieser Austausch erfolgte an drei verschiedenen Stellen im Garten.

Vorhandene Pflanzen, wie Pflaumenbäume, *Sarasouju,* Azaleen, Walnußbäume und *Osmanthus,* wurden wegen der in den Jahreszeiten wechselnden Färbung erhalten.

Das Gesamtbild ändert sich auch während des Morgens und Nachmittags, und mit abendlicher Beleuchtung nach beendeter Arbeit ist der Garten ein gemütlicher Platz. Die Lichter können verändert werden und zusätzlich Musik eingespielt werden, dann verwandelt sich der Garten in eine völlig andere Welt. Ein Gartenliebhaber, der selbst im Garten Hand anlegt, kann ihn in einen für die ganze Familie gemütlichen Platz verwandeln und eine schönere Umgebung für sein Haus schaffen.

Mr. Kumagai is a textile designer, active both in Japan and overseas. The garden of his home was originally used for garden parties, but upon renovating the home he wished to remake it as a Japanese garden which might be enjoyed in a variety of ways, including as a meditative space.

The garden was conceptualized as three circular spaces, two of white sand, the third as a water basin. The circle expresses the infinite, while the ripples of the water and the crests on the sand symbolize extension, thereby effecting the broadening of this limited space.

The water basin is *shigaraki* pottery, and can therefore be moved as so desired. The circle is also an easier space to utilize than the square, and thus useful as a gathering place. The water basin also serves as a *tsukubai*, supplying water for tea-making. The movement of water on the surface of the basin can be viewed from the stepping stones, or the *nobedan*, which lead over the sand. The garden may be enjoyed from the original house, which stands to the north of the garden, or from the newly added main residence to the east, or from the garden chairs to the south.

The garden is surrounded by trees and shrubbery, with the openness of the garden created by the apposition of trees and shrubbery along the wall. Between the house and the new residence the cut stepping stones become natural stones, in order to enhance the rounded effect, and this change takes place in three places around the garden.

Existing trees, including plum, *sarasouju*, azaleas, maples and

熊谷邸庭園
The Kumagai home garden

2. Der Garten von der Halle aus betrachtet. The garden as seen from the waiting room.

3. Gesamtansicht des Gartens. Die Fläche ist schmal, doch die Sandflächen schaffen Raum im Garten.
A full view of the garden. The area is small, but the sand area enhances the feeling of space.

osmanthus, were left in the garden for the seasonal flavoring they offer. The garden is basically small, but by moving about and changing perspectives it takes on different aspects, and can be enjoyed in different ways. The scenes also change between morning and afternoon, and detailed lighting makes it an enjoyable space in the evening, after work is finished. As an additional touch the lighting sources can be moved about and adjusted to complement music, thereby offering a completely different ambience from the daytime. A garden lover who dedicates himself to his garden can make it a place for the whole family to enjoy, and create a better environment in his home.

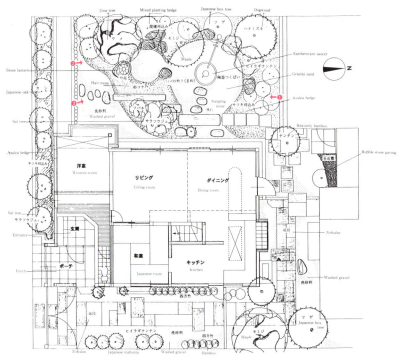

Grundrißplan   Ground plan

Design: Saburo Sone. **Construction:** Sone Landscape Architecture Co.; 1988. **Area:** 120 square meters. **Location:** Kita-ku, Kyoto, Kyoto Pref.

浄妙寺庭園
Jomyo-ji Temple Garden

1. Gesamtansicht des Gartens, aus der Halle betrachtet.

Kamakura liegt in der Nähe einer großen Metropole und ist das Herz der Zen-Kultur. Von hier aus verbreiteten sich seine Lehren in die Städte und die Planung des *Kisenan* Gartens beinhaltet diese Tatsache. Heimische Bäume, Blumen und Steine aus *Kamakura* wurden so viel wie möglich verwendet. Der Garten repräsentiert die Zen-Kultur in vollem Maße. Für die Gebäude im Garten verwendete man vorhandene Materialien, angelehnt an den Landschaftsbau in *Kyoto*. Unser Ziel war es, eine Szenerie zu schaffen, die die Seele des Betrachters beruhigt, indem sie die Schlichtheit *Kamakuras* mit der Kultiviertheit *Kyotos* verknüpft. Das Gebäude wird *Kisenan* genannt und wurde renoviert, um die Schönheit des Gartens während einer gepflegten Tasse Tee zu genießen. Der *Kamakura* Stein ist weich, gehört jedoch zum Ambiente des *Kamakura*, und es ist sehr angenehm, darauf zu laufen. Der Weg führt zum *Kisenan*. Von hier aus ist der Blick auf den Garten wunderschön. Um ein echtes Teehaus zu bauen, wurde neben der Veranda ein Wasserbecken aus Stein errichtet. Außerdem rundet eine *Yunoki* Steinlaterne an einer Ecke des Gebäudes das Gesamtbild ab. Der Ausblick der im Teehaus sitzenden Gäste wurde auch bei der Gestaltung der Fläche mitberücksichtigt. Gegenüber des Wasserbeckens neben der Veranda ist ein Waschbecken und darauf befindet sich ein Glockenspiel, das wunderschöne Geräusche in die Stille einbringt. Vornehmlich sind Zedern und Zedern-Moos gepflanzt, aber auch andere Blumen und Büsche bringen Veränderung während der Jahreszeiten. Der Garten ist so angelegt, daß die Büsche entlang des Weges nicht vom Haus aus zu sehen sind. Eine große japanische Zypresse im mittleren Teil des Gartens ist von *Ume Mansaku, Yamaboushi, Dogwood,* Azaleen, Altheen, Salisbury und anderen Bäumen und Blumen umgeben, die den Wechsel der Jahreszeiten anzeigen.

2. Blick von der Veranda in den hinteren Teil des Gartens mit dem Steinwaschbecken rechts im Vordergrund.

1. A full view of the garden from the center of the hall.
2. A view from the verandah towards the rear of the garden, with the stone wash basin in the right foreground.
3. The view from the garden looking toward the hall.

Design: Saburo Sone. **Construction:** Sone Landscape Architecture Co.; 1991. **Area:** 487 square meters. **Location:** Kamakura, Kanagawa Pref.

浄妙寺庭園
Jomyo-ji temple garden

3. Blick vom Garten in Richtung Halle.

Kamakura is situated next to a major metropolis, and yet retains its natural surroundings. It is the heart of Zen culture, from which these teachings spread to the cities, and the planning for Kisenan garden included such considerations. As much as possible the native trees, flowers and stone of Kamakura were used, and the garden was designed to offer the full flavor of a Zen garden.

For the garden-building we worked with the available materials, applying the landscape techniques of Kyoto. Our aim was to create a scene that soothed the soul of the viewer, offering the simplicity of Kamakura which matches the refinement of Kyoto. The building, called the Kisenan, was refurbished for the occasion, so that one may enjoy the beauty of the garden while drinking tea.

The entrance is paved with slab, the main walkway with flagstones formed of native Kamakura stone and *Ise* cobblestones. The Kamakura rock is soft, but it is part of the ambience of Kamakura, and is enjoyable to walk upon while approaching Kisenan and viewing the garden.

In order to make a proper teahouse a stone water basin formation was built by the verandah, and a *Yunoki* stone lantern added, creating a balanced weight at the corner of the building. The perspective of the people sitting in the teahouse was also considered when designing this area, so that it has the effect of broadening the background vista.

Opposite the water basin by the verandah is a wash basin, and on it is a water chime, which makes a beautiful sound in the silence.

The plants are primarily cedars and cedar moss, as well as other flowers and shrubs which can be enjoyed through the seasons. The garden is laid out so that those strolling the paths are not seen from the building. There is a large Japanese cypress in the middle of the garden which has been surrounded with ume *mansaku*, *yamaboushi*, dogwood, azalea, althea, salisbury and other trees and flowers that announce the changing seasons. The backdrop of the roof of the main hall, and the hills, has the effect of heightening the scene.

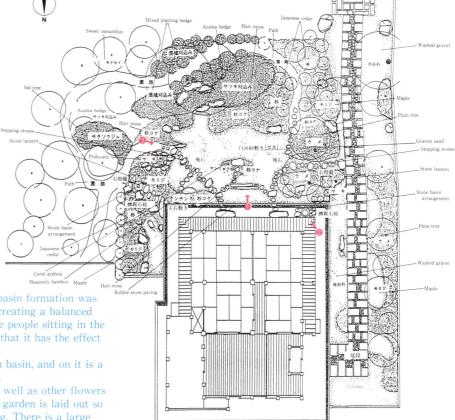

Grundrißplan   Ground plan

明月院庭園
Meigetsu-in Temple Garden

1. Gesamtansicht der *Mt. Shumisen* Formation im Hauptgarten. Die Berge im Hintergrund bringen Natürlichkeit in den Garten.

Der *Meigetsu-in* Tempel ist als *Hydrangeas* Tempel berühmt, und während der *Hydrangea*-Zeit kommen sehr viele Besucher. Es wurde ein Plan entworfen, den Besuchern einen schöneren Blick auf die Blumen auf dem Grundstück zu ermöglichen. Die Blumen, Bäume und Wege im Inneren des *Nakamon* wurden zu einem im Zen-Stil erbauten Garten umgebaut, angelehnt an die bekannte *Kamakura* Atmosphäre.

Hydrangeas verändern ihr Aussehen während der Frühlings- und Wintermonate. Nun, da es sich um einen Zen-Tempel handelt, aus dem man auf den Garten blickt, um die Zeit zu vergessen, bietet dieser Garten viele Attraktionen. Manche Besucher nehmen einen langen Weg auf sich, um die Blumen (Lotus, *Kaido* Kirsche und japanische *Allspice*) im *Meigetsu-in* und die Felsenformationen zu bewundern. Die *Shumisen* Formation aus *Ibiishi* Granit gestaltet den Hintergrund und ist von hohen Hecken und Blumen umgeben. Diese Hecken verdecken den Blick auf vorbeilaufende Passanten auf dem dahinterliegenden Weg. Bevor die *Shumisen* Formation mit weißem Sand aufgeschüttet wurde, war sie ein „Platz der Zeit". In dieses Meer aus Sand ragt eine Halbinsel, welche die Felsenformation noch unterstreicht. Auf dieser Halbinsel befindet sich eine mit einer Rot-Pinie besetzte Kranichinsel. Die Rot-Pinie ist sehr häufig in diesem Gebiet – in dem Fall verbindet sie die Berge mit dem Garten. Der Garten des *Hydrangeas* Tempels unterstreicht die Schönheit der Natur. Die Lotus-Blüten sind eine weitere Attraktion im Garten, und wenn man den schmalen Weg durch den Bambus-Hain geht, kann man wilde *Hydrangeas* und tandere Blumen und Bäume sehen, wie sie in früheren Zeiten ausgesehen haben. Für die Felsenformationen wurden heimische Blausteine und *Ibiishi* Granit verwendet. Jeder Stein hat seine eigene Form und wurde deshalb an adäquater Stelle eingesetzt. Die Felsen in den Formationen haben die Form eines geöffneten Fächers und vermitteln gleichzeitig die natürliche Schönheit *Kamakuras*.

2. Die *Mt. Shumisen* Felsenformation und die geschnittenen Hecken im Mittelteil des Gartens.

須弥山の庭
Shumisen Garden

3. Diagonalblick durch den Hauptgarten mit der Kranich- und Schildkröteninsel im Vordergrund.

1. A full view of the Mt. Shumisen formation of the main garden. The mountains to the rear offer a natural backdrop to the scene.
2. The Shumisen rock formation and the trimmed shrubbery at the center of the garden.
3. A diagonal view of the main garden, with the crane and turtle stones in the foreground.

Meigetsu-in Temple is famous as the temple of hydrangeas, and during the hydrangea season there are many visitors. A plan was undertaken to offer visitors an even more satisfying view of the flowers inside the grounds. The flowers, trees and paths of the area inside the *nakamon* were rearranged to create a Zen-style garden, as well as one highly evocative of the Kamakura atmosphere.

Hydrangeas offer a completely different view from spring to winter. And yet, as a Zen temple from which to view a garden and forget time, this garden offers numerous attractions.

People have long come to enjoy the flowers of Meigetsu-in—lotus, *kaido* cherry and Japanese allspice—and the rock formations. The Shumisen formation, created from ibiishi granite, is seen in the background, surrounded by tall hedged trees and flowers, which have the effect of masking strollers on the nearby path. In this way the mountain in the background becomes a dynamic "following space," making the view from the main hall panoramic.

Before the Shumisen formation is an area of white sand serving as the "space of time". Into this ocean of sand juts a peninsula, which accentuates the mountain formation, and there is a crane island topped with a red pine, a specie found in the local hills, and this likewise adds to the image of continuous mountains. The garden of the temple of hydrangeas is thus especially fine for appreciating nature.

The lotus blossoms are another beautiful aspect of this garden, and when taking the small path through the bamboo grove one has an opportunity to see hydrangeas in the wild and other flowers and trees as they looked during the days of the old capital. Seen through the changing seasons the dry waterfall, centered on the Shumisen formation, offers much to be appreciated.

For the rock formations local bluestone and *ibiishi* granite were used. Every rock has its own flavor, and here the stones have all been used differently. The rocks in the formations of the succeeding space resemble the bullseye of an open fan, further suggesting the natural beauty of Kamakura.

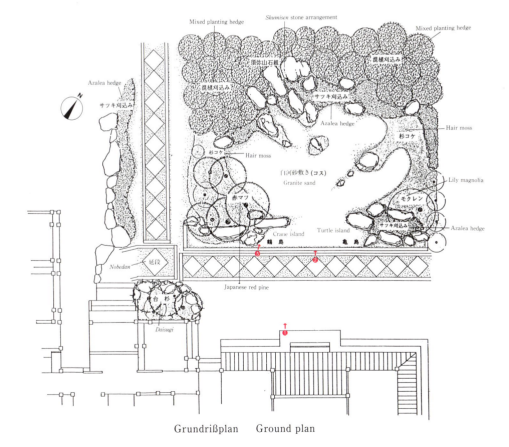

Grundrißplan   Ground plan

裏庭
The rear garden

4. Steinweg und Granit-*Nobedan* des hinteren Gartens der Haupthalle.

5. Steinweg und *Nobedan* führen zum Teehaus.

4. The stepping stones and granite nobedan of the main hall's rear garden.
5. The stepping stones and nobedan extending toward the teahouse.
6. A view of the stone water basin from beside the guest quarters.
7. The garden and teahouse as seen from the study.
8. A full view of the rear garden from the stone in front of the stone water basin.

裏庭
The rear garden

Der Garten hinter der Haupthalle führt die Gehwege mit einem Steinweg und einem *Nobedan* zusammen. Die durch das Gebäude und die *Dodan* Azaleenhecke gebildete Fläche ist mit einer gewundenen Linie moosbewachsener Steine ausgelegt. Die roten Steine des Weges stammen aus *Omori, Kyoto* und bilden gegen das grüne Moos und den weißen Sand einen starken Kontrast. In diesem schlichten Arrangement sind die Steine und der *Nobedan* offensichtlich in einem bestimmten Rhythmus angelegt. Das Wasserbecken am Teehaus ist aus *Kurama* Stein (schwarzer *Mica*-Granit aus *Kyoto*), der sich stark von den Steinen um das Teehaus abhebt. Hier sind die Steine mit grünem Moos bewachsen, am Teehaus gehen sie in braunen *Kurama* Stein über. In der Gartengestaltung ist es wichtig, sich naturfarbenen Materials zu bedienen. Dicke Baumstämme schaffen auch eine angenehme Atmosphäre im Garten vor dem Teehaus.

The garden behind the main hall serves to draw together the walkway to the teahouse and the mountain scenery in the background by way of stepping stones and a *nobedan*. The space created by the building and the hedge of dodan azaleas is complemented with a curved border of moss-covered stones. The redstone stepping stones are from Omori, Kyoto, and along with the green moss, stand out in sharp contrast to the white sand space. In this simple arrangement the stepping stones and *nobedan* achieve a palpable rhythm.

The water basin by the teahouse is made of *kurama* stone, a black mica granite from Kyoto, which blends with the stepping stones around the teahouse. Here the stepping stones are covered with green moss, and as one approaches the teahouse, they change to the brown *kurama* stone. In garden-building it is important to make wise use of the natural coloring of materials. The thick trunks of the garden plants add further to the appreciation of those enjoying the garden from the teahouse.

6. Blick auf das Steinwasserbecken von den Gästezimmern aus.

7. Der Garten und das Teehaus vom Lehrzimmer aus betrachtet.

8. Gesamtansicht des hinteren Gartens vom Stein vor dem Wasserbecken aus betrachtet.

Design: Saburo Sone. **Construction:** Sone Landscape Architecture Co.; 1990. **Area:** 655 square meters. **Location:** Kamakura, Kanagawa Pref.

宗安寺庭園
Soan-ji Temple Garden

1. Gesamtansicht des Hauptgartens aus dem Lehrzimmer.

2. Blick auf den Mittelteil des Gartens mit dem trockenen Wasserfall.

Garden Elements

The appearance of stone lanterns and stone water basins in gardens dates from the early Edo period, and shows the influence of the teahouse garden.

When placing these elements in the garden there is a simple rule: if it is a stone lantern, it must not be a carelessly purchased piece. In fact, it should be able to stand alone as a work of art. In order to recognize a good piece one needs to study and observe many examples of good works. At minimum, one should avoid the use of mass produced, inexpensive items.

Today in Japan the number of stone masons capable of creating high quality stone artifices is decreasing, and there is a strong reliance on products from China and Korea. Unfortunately, problems with the design blueprints for the orders have resulted in very few examples that can be called good. I make every effort to create an accurate blueprint and use only the best technicians for these items. (Yoshikawa)

宗安寺庭園
Soan-ji temple garden

4. Das Naturstein-Wasserbecken im Garten.

3. Der trockene Wasserfall und das Steinwasserbecken, die Hauptelemente des Gartens.

Zusammen mit der Renovierung des Lehrzimmers wurde ein Plan ausgearbeitet, den Teegarten daran anschließen zu lassen. Da sich direkt hinter dem Grundstück Berge befinden, beschloß man, eine niedrige Erdmauer zu bauen, um die natürliche Umgebung des Gartens beizubehalten. Ein trockener Wasserfall mit dichten Büschen besetzt und ein Waschbecken aus Stein bilden eine Formation. Der Wasserfall paßt sich sehr schön in das hügelige Tal ein, während die in der Mitte stehenden Elemente wie Wasserbecken und Laterne die hier flache Landschaft unterstreichen. Links im Garten finden sich eine Kranichinsel-Formation und gepflanzte Pinien. Da der Garten auf erhöhtem Grund erbaut ist, kann man die Pinien schon vom Parkplatz aus sehen. Die meisten Steine und Formationen stammen aus den umliegenden Bergen. Der rote Stein der Kranichinsel und verschiedene andere Steine sind Geschenke von den Gemeindemitgliedern des Tempels. Als die Grube für den Hausbau ausgehoben wurde, fand man eine große Steinplatte, die im Garten als Zierstein wieder auftaucht. Der trockene Wasserfall ist aus *Sanzon* Steinen erbaut, wobei ein Stein als Basis dient und die Vorstellung von fallendem Wasser verstärkt. Mittig vor dem Wasserfall wurde ein Stein plaziert, der eine sich stromaufwärts fortbewegende Schildkröte darstellt. Das in Gartenmitte aufgebaute Waschbecken aus Stein paßt sich in die Landschaft ein, so daß nur die Steinlaterne Akzente setzt. Die Laterne ist aus *"far mountain"* Stein und wurde hier aufgestellt, um das Auge auch auf den Hintergrund aufmerksam zu machen. In der linken Hälfte des Gartens stehen ein Walnußbaum, ein *Horuto* und Kamelien, die eine Verbindung zu den Bäumen auf den Bergen schaffen. Die einzig anderen Bäume, die gepflanzt wurden, waren Pinien. Die mit weißem Sand aufgefüllte Fläche ist schmal, doch gut gepflegt, und stellt die Menschheit in einer kargen Umgebung dar.

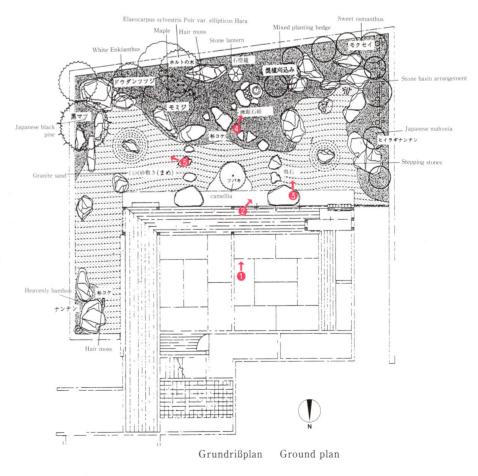

Grundrißplan   Ground plan

1. A view of the main garden from within the study.
2. A view of the garden centered on the dry waterfall.
3. The dry waterfall and stone water basin, the main elements of the garden.
4. The garden's natural stone water basin.

111

宗安寺庭園
Soan-ji temple garden

5. Die Kranich-Felsenformation, die gegenüber der Schildkröteninsel und dem trockenen Wasserfall steht.
The crane rock formation, which stands opposite the turtle rock and dry waterfall formation.

Together with the reconstruction of the study, a plan was put forth to create a tea garden adjacent to it. Mountains rise directly to the rear, so it was decided to build a low earthen wall to pull together the natural scenery and the lines of the garden, adding a dry mountain and water formation as the central attraction, with a stone wash basin and cropped shrubs by the dry waterfall. The latter provides continuity with the mountain valley, while the stone water basin and lantern, situated in the middle ground, maintain the overall low profile of the landscape. On the left side of the area a crane island rock formation was laid, and pines planted.

Because the garden is built on high ground, these pines can be seen from the temple parking lot. The view from indoors is important, but here the scene from the road and parking area was considered, as well.

Most of the scenic rocks and formation stones were taken from the local mountains. The redstone of the crane island, and several other stones, were presents from parishoners of the temple. When the site was excavated for the construction of the building a large slab was removed, and this too was used as a scenic stone in the garden.

The dry waterfall formation was made to resemble the sanzon stones, and a stone was laid at the base of the waterfall to deepen the image of the falls. In the middle foreground of the falls lies a rock expressing a turtle heading upstream. The stone wash basin, situated in the middle of the garden, is not part of the scenery from within, so that the only accent to the setting is provided by the stone lantern. The stone by the lantern is a 'far mountain' stone, set there to draw the eye into the background, while the stepping stones and moss of the clear area add breadth to the garden as a whole.

To the left of the center stands maple, *horuto* and camellias, providing a connection with the trees on the mountains. The only other planting was the stand of pines.

The area of white sand is small, but with grooming it suggests the pulsation of man in an austere environment.

Overall, this is a flat-style garden, designed to offer a different picture depending on the angle from which one looks.

Design: Saburo Sone. **Construction:** Sone Landscape Architecture Co.; 1989. **Area:** 70 square meters. **Location:** Kochi, Kochi Pref.

ホテル磯部ガーデン
Garden of the Isobe Hotel

Pond garden

1. Gesamtansicht des Teichs im Garten. Das Brunnenwasser fließt aus der Felsenformation in den Teich.

Das *Isobe* Hotel ist bekannt als *Shitakiri Suzume Inn* (aus dem Volksmärchen: Vom Mann, der das Schwalbenhaus besucht), und deshalb wurde *Mosochiku,* eine Art Bambus, in dem Schwalben leben, gepflanzt.

Dieser Garten ist auf einem Grundstück angelegt, das man von allen Seiten her einsehen kann; den schönsten Blick erlangt man aus der vorderen Lobby. Im hinteren Teil des Gartens ist ein trockener Wasserfall aus blauen Steinen der nahen *Gunma* Präfektur, von dem sich ein Fluß in Richtung Lobby ausbreitet. Ein Waschbecken im Vordergrund verstärkt den Eindruck von fließendem Wasser. Darüber hinaus liegt ein Stein in Schildkrötenform im Sand, und es scheint, als ob sie flußaufwärts schwimmen würde. Östlich der Lobby links ist der Garten mit einem Teich angelegt. Dadurch ändert sich das von der Lobby aus einzusehende Bild ganz plötzlich. Vor dem Teich steht eine Formation aus Felsen, die auch den Brunnen sehr schön umrundet. Besonders bei Nacht ist dies ein schöner Anblick, wenn die Wasserblasen wie Edelsteine erscheinen. Südlich des Teichs befindet sich ein Sandstrand, und auf der Halbinsel steht eine neue *Misaki* Steinlaterne.

Weiter um den linken Teil des Teichs gelangt man in den Garten vor dem Badehaus. Dieser Garten beinhaltet eine trockene Felsenformation und geschnittene Büsche, um einen „geschlossenen" Gartenstil zu erhalten. Dieser trockene Wasserfall ist teilweise aus *Sanmon* Blausteinen erbaut und erstreckt sich in eine Ecke (Seite an Seite). Der Garten dient zur Abkühlung für Gäste des Badehauses. Es ist gegenüber der Lobby gebaut und gibt den Blick auf den südlichen Teil des Gartens frei. Dieses Hotel bietet seinen Gästen „Erholung im Grünen" und erfreut durch verschiedene Themen im Garten. Um die Flächen nahe dem Gebäude lebendig zu gestalten, wurden gerade wachsender Bambus und Zedern gepflanzt und mit kurvig wachsenden geschnittenen Büschen am Boden kombiniert.

2. Gesamtansicht des Gartens aus dem obersten Stockwerk betrachtet.

1. A full view of the pond and garden. Spring water flows from the rock formation of the well into the pond.
2. A full view of the garden as seen from the upper stairs.

池泉の庭
Pond garden

3. Sandstrand, trockener Fluß und Wasserfall, aus der Lobby betrachtet.

4. Eine Seitenansicht des Sandstrands.

5. Blick auf den Teich vom Weg aus dem mittleren Teil des Gartens.

6. Felsenformation am Brunnen, der den Teich mit Wasser speist.

In der Mitte des Elements steht eine Felsenformation, die zusätzlich Gewicht in das Arrangement bringt. Der Wasserfall, der von der Lobby aus ganz hinten im Garten zu erkennen ist, und der vom Badehaus zu sehende sind ein und derselbe Wasserfall. Er wirkt jedoch durch die verschiedenen Blickwinkel absolut verschieden. Normalerweise sind von hohen Häusern eingefaßte Gärten sehr dunkel, doch der weiße Sand des trockenen Flusses erhellt die Fläche. Im Garten ist ein Weg angebracht, auf dem die Gäste durch die Anlage laufen können.

Da die Gäste den Garten aus allen Winkeln betrachten können, muß jeder Teil der Formationen für sich interessant sein. Der Garten bietet einige Attraktionen, wie z.B. der sich im Bambus fangende Wind, der Klang des Wassers und die Farben der Blumen. Dieser Garten soll den Reisenden helfen, dem Alltagsstreß zu entkommen, und die Erfahrung der Natur soll ihre fünf Sinne schärfen.

The Hotel Isobe is known as the *shitakiri suzume* inn (from the folktale about the man who visits the home of the swallows), and for that reason *mosochiku*, a kind of bamboo where the swallows lived, was planted.

This garden is situated in an area which can be viewed from all directions, with the setting designed for viewing from the front lobby. In the back of the garden is the dry waterfall, made of local Gumma prefecture bluestone, from which a stream spreads out towards the forefront, towards the lobby. There is a wash basin in the foreground, reinforcing the impression that this imaginary water is flowing. Moreover, a rock resembling a turtle lies in the sand, and may be seen as swimming upstream. Walking to the east of the lobby, to the left, the garden becomes a pond garden, changing dramatically from what is seen from the front of the lobby. In the front of the pond stands the formation of rocks surrounding the well spring, and this, when illuminated at night, has the appearance of bubbling forth with gemstones. To the south of the pond is a sand beach, and on the peninsula stands a new *misaki* stone lantern.

Continuing around to the left of the pond garden one enters the garden before the bathhouse. This garden contains a dry rock formation and trimmed bushes for a close-in scenic garden style.

枯山水の庭
Karesansui garden

7. Blick auf den trockenen Wasserfall und Fluß von der Lobby aus betrachtet. Das Wasser im Waschbecken strahlt Kraft aus.

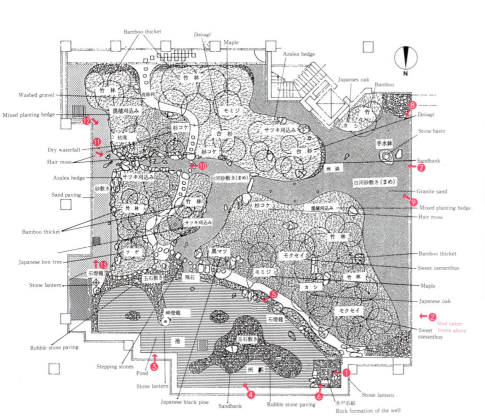

Grundrißplan   Ground plan

8. Der Vorgarten von der Lobby aus betrachtet.

3. The sand beach, dry stream and waterfall as seen from the lobby.
4. A lateral perspective on the sand beach.
5. A view of the pond garden from the path of the central garden.
6. The rock formation of the well, which supplies the pond with water.
7. A view of the dry waterfall and stream from the lobby. The water in the wash basin lends force to the illusion of water.
8. The front garden as seen from the lobby.

115

枯山水の庭
Karesansui garden

9. Der Felsen der Schildkröteninsel scheint flußaufwärts in Richtung Felsenformation und trockenem Wasserfall zu schwimmen.

This dry waterfall likewise uses *sanzon* bluestone for its material, and stretches out in a narrow, side to side configuration. This garden serves as the cooling area for the bathhouse, and stands on the opposite of the lobby, affording a southern view of the area. For guests, this hotel offers a chance to relax in green surroundings, and to enjoy the various scenes of the garden.

In order to bring to life the space of a garden enclosed by a tall building, straight-growing bamboo and cedars were planted, with curved, trimmed shrubbery planted over the low ground. In the midst of these elements, the rock formation serves to add weight. The rock waterfall which is seen in the far background from the lobby, and the one which is seen from the bathhouse, are both of the same formation, but from two sides, appear as distinct scenes. Normally, gardens enclosed by tall buildings are dark for lack of sunlight, but here the white sand of the dry stream serves to lighten the space.

Inside the garden there is a path, so that guests may walk through the garden. While people can view the garden from any angle, each view must be impressive in its own right. The garden offers various sensations, be it the bamboo whispering in the wind, the sound of the water, or the color of the flowers. It is hoped that this is a garden that will offer the traveler who is escaping his daily life a chance to experience nature with all of his five senses.

10. Der „feuchte" Steinweg, der einen Teil der Felsenformation des trockenen Wasserfalls ausmacht.

枯山水の庭
Karesansui garden

11. Der Wasserfall von der Lobby aus betrachtet, dahinter liegt das Badehaus.

12. Der Wasserfall vor dem Badehaus. Dazu verwendet wurde Blaustein aus heimischen Bergen.

13. Der Wasserfall vor dem Badehaus vom Sandstrand des Gartens aus betrachtet.

9. The turtle rock appears to be swimming upstream in the direction of the dry rock formation and waterfall.
10. The 'wet' stepping stones, which form part of the rock formation at the dry waterfall.
11. The dry waterfall as seen from the lobby. Beyond it is the bathhouse.
12. The waterfall formation in front of the bathhouse. Local bluestone was used in the construction.
13. The waterfall formation in front of the bathhouse as seen from the garden's sand beach.

Design: Saburo Sone. **Construction:** Sone Landscape Architecture Co.; 1989. **Area:** 560 square meters. **Location:** Annaka, Gunma Pref.

佐々木邸庭園
The Sasaki Home Garden

1. Weg zum Haupteingang des Hauses durch das Haupttor betrachtet. Der Weg ist von *Kokumazasa* Bambusgras und Moos eingefaßt.

2. Parkplatz aus Granitsteinen; das Dach des Haupttors ist mit Zypressen-Zweigen gedeckt.

3. Alte im *Omi* Stil erbaute Steinlaterne im Vorgarten.

4. Zylindrisches Steinbecken mit sorgfältig gepflanztem Moos.

Im Layout des *Sasaki Home* Gartens wurde berücksichtigt, daß an das Gebäude ein Bürohaus und ein Parkplatz angebunden sind. Deshalb waren zwei Wege zum Haupteingang und zum Hintereingang nötig. Das Dach des Haupttors ist mit Zypressen-Zweigen gedeckt. Um eine Einheit zu schaffen, wählte der Designer einen Granitboden für den Parkplatz vor dem Tor. Ein Weg aus geschnittenen Platten führt vom Tor zum um die Ecke liegenden Hauseingang. Der Weg ist von außen durch einen *Cryptomeria* Sichtschutzzaun eingefaßt und innen zum Haus hin mit einem Bambuszaun abgeschirmt. Hinter dem Innentor, das zwischen Haupttor und Eingang steht, ist der Vorgarten angelegt. Er beinhaltet japanische Rot-Pinien, im *Kitayama*-Stil geschnittene *Cryptomeria* und Pflaumenbäume.

Genau in der Mitte und direkt vor dem Eingang steht eine *Kawageta* Steinlaterne. Das wunderbar gepflegte Haarmoos auf dieser Fläche zeigt deutlich, wie sehr der Eigentümer auf einen gepflegten Garten Wert legt.

Der Hauptgarten ist entlang des Hauses gegenüber dem Haupttor als schmaler Garten angelegt. Die Fläche beinhaltet ein *Suikinkutsu*, das einen Teil des *Tsukubai* Arrangements darstellt, und das Haarmoos als Bodenbepflanzung läßt den Garten hochwertiger aussehen. Das offene Viertel des Bambuszauns am äußeren Rand des Gartens schafft zusätzlich Raum, und die wenigen dünnen gekreuzten Bambusstäbe machen das Design noch interessanter. Der Zaun ist ca. 25 m lang. Er hat keine Stützpfeiler, und Grundpfeiler stehen in 1,8 m kurzen Abständen.

佐々木邸庭園
The Sasaki home garden

5. Hauptgarten mit Fliesenweg und hellgrüner Bepflanzung, Granitstufen und schlichter Bodenbepflanzung aus Haarmoos, gewaschenem Schotter, *Misaki* Steinlaterne, und im Hintergrund führt eine Bambus-Wasserpfeife zu einem Steinbecken.

Diese Pfeiler bestehen aus mit *Cryptomeria* Zweigen ummantelten Beton, und die Bambus-Stangen sind daran festgenagelt. Andere Merkmale im Garten sind unter anderem ein paar Ziersteine (keine Arrangements), Bäume, die den Ausgleich zwischen dem Gebäude und dem Garten schaffen, und zuletzt noch die rustikal ausgewählte Bodenbepflanzung (rustikal auf Wunsch des Eigentümers). Schließlich wurde der Teil links neben dem Haupttor, der zum Hintereingang führt, teilweise mit Granitsand aufgefüllt und durch Haarmoos und einen *Kinkakuji* Zaun eingefaßt. In der Ecke ist eine im *Sode* Stil erbaute Laterne, und ein Steinweg führt zurück in den Hauptgarten.

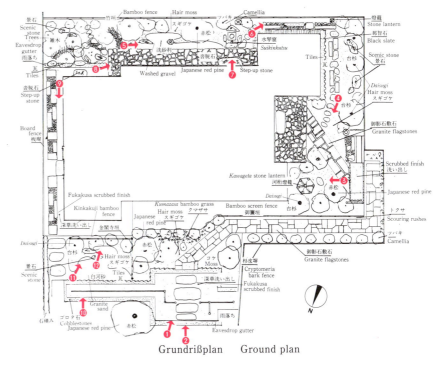

1. Pathway to the main entrance to the house, seen through the main outer gate. The path is bordered by *kokumazasa* bamboo grass and moss.
2. Granite-paved parking lot, gate roof covered with cypress bark, and surrounding plants, including pines and azaleas.
3. Old Omi-style stone lantern in the front garden.
4. Cylindrical stone basin, with carefully "sculpted" moss.
5. Main garden, with flagstone path of light green andesite, biotite granite step-up stone, simple ground cover of hair moss, washed gravel, *misaki* stone lantern, and, in the background, a bamboo water pipe leading to a stone basin.

佐々木邸庭園
The Sasaki home garden

6. Bambuszaun mit offener Zeile, nur von Bambusstücken gestützt.

7. *Ginkakuji Tsukubai* Arrangement und *Suikinkutsu*, ein perfekter Ausblick.

8. Die großen Traufen des Hauses sind im Stil der Tee-Zeremonienhäuser gebaut.

The laying out of the garden of the Sasaki home accompanied the addition of an office to the main house and the construction of a parking lot and two paths, from the main gate to the back entrance and to the front door of the house. The main gate has a cypress bark roof; to harmonize with this, the designer selected a granite stone pavement for the parking lot outside the gate. A cut-stone pathway leads from the gate to the house entrance around the corner. The path is bordered by a cryptomeria bark fence on the outside and a bamboo screen fence between it and the house. Beyond the inner gate, which stands between the main gate and the house entrance, is the front garden, an area planted with Japanese red pines, Kitayama cut cryptomerias, and plum trees. Amid these and directly in front of the entrance is an appropriately placed *kawageta* stone lantern. The beautifully manicured hair moss in this area also clearly indicates the care with which the owner takes care of his garden.

The main garden is a long, narrow area on the side of the house opposite the main gate. This area includes a *suikinkutsu*, which is part of a *tsukubai* arrangement, and a ground cover of hair moss makes the narrow garden look more expansive. The empty second tier of the four-tiered bamboo fence on the outer boundary of the garden also adds a sense of spaciousness, and the few thin pieces of bamboo crisscrossing makes the open space a bit more interesting. The fence is some twenty-five meters long because the garden is so narrow; bracing posts had to be eliminated and the support posts placed only 1.8 meters apart. These posts are made of concrete wrapped with cryptomeria bark, and the bamboo pieces are nailed to these.

Other features of the garden include the use of a few scenic stones (but no stone arrangements), trees that enhance the balance between the house and the garden, and the use of rustic-appearing ground cover, in accordance with the wishes of the owner. Finally, the section of the garden to the left of the main gate, leading to the back entrance, includes an area of granite sand surrounded by a border of hair moss and a Kinkakuji fence. In the corner is a *sode*-style lantern, and a stone pathway leads back to the main garden.

Design: Shin'ichi Kosuge (Teibo). **Construction:** Shin'ichi Kosuge, Akiyoshi Toyama, Kisaburo Aida; 1987. **Area:** 500 square meters. **Location:** Ichihara, Chiba Pref.

佐々木邸庭園
The Sasaki home garden

9. Steinplatten zwischen Haus- und Gartenmauer führen vom Hintereingang zum Hauptgarten.

10. Blick vom Hintergeingang; der Steinweg auf Bild 9 führt raus zum Parkplatz.

11. Der kleine Garten links neben dem Haupteingang mit Granitsand und dem *Kinkakuji* Zaun.

12. Laterne im *Sode* Stil steht im kleinen Garten auf Moos.

6. Bamboo fence with open area crisscrossed with thin pieces of bamboo.
7. Ginkakuji *tsukubai* arrangement and *suikinkutsu*, a perfect view from one of the windows of the house.
8. The wide eaves of the house are in the style of a tea ceremony house; the various trees planted nearby enhance the otherwise narrow garden's sense of spaciousness.
9. Stone-paved narrow area between the house and garden wall, leading from the back entrance of the main garden.
10. View from the back door; the stone pathway in Figure 9 leads via the cut-stone path shown here (*left*) out to the parking lot.
11. The small garden to the left of the main entrance, with its granite sand and Kinkakuji fence.
12. *Sode*-style stone lantern in the moss of the small garden.

岡野邸庭園
The Okano Home Garden

1. Der Mittelteil des Gartens vom Vordereingang des Hauses betrachtet. Das Drei-Stein-Arrangement links im Vordergrund bringt zusätzlich Tiefe für den Wasserfall im Hintergrund.

Der Garten des *Okano Homes* ist als Trockengarten unter Verwendung von *Biotit*-Granit (sehr häufig in Gärten verwendet) gebaut. Obwohl viele dieser Steine ähnlich aussehen, fanden wir Steine mit unterschiedlicher Form, um einen interessanten Anblick zu schaffen. Durch den Garten führt eine Straße zu der Garage im hinteren Teil des Hauses; typisch für diese Gegend in Japan. Dies erfordert eine sorgfältige Planung. Die Straße wurde in das Design aufgenommen. Sie stellt den Wasserkörper im Garten dar. Die Granitfliesen des Weges und die Mauern aus Naturstein auf beiden Seiten sind in sanften Kurven angelegt, um leicht von der Straße aus am Haus vorbei zum Eingang zu gelangen.

Im Vorgarten (die Fläche zwischen Gartentor und Hauseingang) wurde gleich vor dem im japanischen Stil errichteten Raum eine kleine kunstvolle Gartenlandschaft errichtet. Direkt gegenüber dem Haus in zentraler Lage ist ein trockener Wasserfall aus hohen Steinen angelegt. Von hier aus fließt ein trockenes Flußbett in Richtung Steinweg am Eingangstor. Vom Eingang des Hauses aus hat man eine schöne Gesamtübersicht über den Garten; ein Drei-Steinarrangement zwischen dem Eingang und dem trockenen Wasserfall verleiht zusätzlich Tiefe. Die Bäume sind z.B. Pinien, *Podocarps Aloeswoods,* Rhododendron, Walnußbäume und Pflaumenbäume.

The garden of the Okano home is a dry-landscape garden employing biotite granite, the kind often used in such gardens. Although many of these stones have basically the same shape curved surfaces meeting at corners we were able to find a variety of stones, resulting in more interesting arrangements. The garden includes a driveway leading to a garage at the back of the house, a layout typical of this area of Japan that requires a careful garden design. The driveway itself was integrated into the design, and laid out in imitation of a body of water. The granite flagstones of the driveway and the natural-face-stone walls on either side are laid out in a gentle curve to allow cars to enter from the road easily and keep the house entrance hidden.

In the front garden (the area from the garden gate to the entrance of the house), a small artificial mountain of rocks was placed directly in front of a Japanese-style room, and directly across from the house in a central position is a vivid dry-waterfall stone arrangement employing tall stones. From this "flows" a dry streambed toward the stone path from the gate. Standing at the entrance to the house, one can take in virtually the whole garden ; a three-stone arrangement between the entrance and the dry waterfall adds a sense of depth to the latter. Garden trees include pines, podocarps, aloeswoods, rhododendrons, maples, and plum trees.

Design: Shin'ichi Kosuge(Teibo). **Construction:** Shin'ichi Kosuge, Kazuo Ebihara, Kiyoshi Fukuda; 1992. **Area:** 600 square meters. **Location:** Yawara, Ibaraki Pref.

岡野邸庭園
The Okano home garden

1. The central part of the garden, viewed from the front entrance to the house. The three-stone arrangement in the left foreground adds a sense of depth to the dry waterfall in the distance.
2. Dry waterfall, the focal point of the garden. The waterfall source stone, the largest in the garden, has an upward slant, rendering a sense of energy.
3. Three-stone arrangement to the right of the dry waterfall. The contrast between the horizontal stone in the center and the small stone in the left foreground adds energy to the arrangement.
4. Three-stone arrangement with a mountain-shaped main stone and a standing accessory stone on the right that could well be considered a turtle head stone in some arrangements.

2. Trockener Wasserfall als Blickfang im Garten. Die Quelle ist der größte Stein im Garten und ragt keilförmig in die Höhe und strahlt Energie aus.

3. Drei-Stein-Arrangement rechts neben dem trockenen Wasserfall. Der Kontrast zwischen dem horizontalen Mittelstein und dem kleinen links im Vordergrund bringt Energie in die Formation.

4. Drei-Stein-Arrangement mit Hauptstein in Bergform. Der Begleitstein rechts daneben kann als Schildkrötenkopf betrachtet werden.

岡野邸庭園
The Okano home garden

5. The approach from the gate to the entrance to the house. The driveway has a wide curve.
6. A corner in the stone wall bordering the driveway. Stones of biotite granite do not usually have flat surfaces like this.
7. Stone arrangement inside the garden gate. The low placement of the stone on the right adds interest.
8. View from the driveway of the dry waterfall, from the opposite side of which "flows" a dry streambed.

5. Der Weg vom Tor zum Eingang des Hauses. Die Straße ist mit einer großen Kurve angelegt.

6. Steine aus *Biotit* Granit haben gewöhnlich keine glatte Oberfläche.

7. Das Steinarrangement im Garten. Der flache Stein rechts ist ein zusätzlicher Blickfang.

8. Blick von der Straße auf den trockenen Wasserfall, von der gegenüberliegenden Seite aus betrachtet.

飯泉邸庭園
The Iizumi Home Garden

1. Gesamtansicht des Gartens. Die Bäume im Mittelgarten sind im *Kitayama* Stil geschnittene *Cryptomeria*.

Das *Iizumi* Grundstück ist ein langes, sich von Nord nach Süd erstreckendes Land. Das Haus steht am nördlichen Ende, und der Garten (als Viereck angelegt) ist zur Straße hin erbaut. Der Parkplatz befindet sich außerhalb des Gartens links neben dem Tor und ist durch eine Mauer aus Natursteinen abgegrenzt; die sich von der rechten Seite in den Garten erstreckenden Büsche bringen Tiefe in den Garten. Der breite Weg vom Gartentor zum Eingang teilt den Garten in zwei unterschiedliche Hälften auf. Der Weg ist leicht geschwungen. Der mittlere Teil des Weges ist von Büschen gesäumt und sichert so die Privatsphäre der Bewohner. Der Raum, der im Westen in den Garten ragt, ist mit einer Feuerstelle ausgestattet und ist deshalb sehr gut für die Tee-Zeremonie geeignet. Seitlich daneben in Richtung Vorderhaus befindet sich eine Terrasse, von der aus ein Steinweg in den Teegarten führt, der von einem modernen, großgekurvten *Koetsu* Zaun eingefaßt ist. Dieser Zaun, das *Shihobutsu* Steinbecken und die *Oribe* Steinlaterne im Teegarten schaffen einen verbindenden Blick von der Terrasse aus. Ein *Katsuraho* Flügelzaun reicht fast bis zum Ende des *Koetsu* Zauns. Östlich des Vorderhauses ist ein Weg aus *Pyroxene Andesite* Steinen. Diese sind in ziemlich großen Abständen ausgelegt und mit *Dwarf Snake's Beard* durchwachsen, um eine leicht zu pflegende Grünfläche zu erhalten.

2. Das Gartentor von außen betrachtet.

3. Die Mauer ist aus Natursteinen und mit einem *Kinkakuji* Zaun versehen.

飯泉邸庭園
The Iizumi home garden

4. Der breite Weg vom Gartentor zum Haus hat kleine Abschnitte aus hellgrüner *Andesite*, die Akzente setzen.

5. Die Vorderseite des Hauses östlich des Eingangs. Die Begrenzung ist aus *Biotit Granit;* die kleinen schwarzen Steine fangen den tropfenden Regen der Traufen auf.

6. *Pyroxene Andesite* Steinweg mit *Dwarf Snake's Beard* bepflanzt.

The Iizumi property is a long north-south piece of land, with the house at the northern end and the garden, essentially a square shape, in front of this and facing the road. The parking area to the left of and outside the gate is separated from the garden by a natural-face-stone wall; shrubbery extends from the right side of the gate into the garden, giving a sense of depth. The wide path from the garden gate to the entrance to the house divides the garden into two sides, but to avoid any sense that there is a separation into two distinct parts, the path bends slightly. Shrubbery lines the middle portion of the path, ensuring the privacy of people in the house.

The room protruding into the garden on the west side of the house contains a fireplace and therefore serves well as a tea ceremony room. To the side of this and against the front of the house is a terrace from which leads a pathway of stepping stones into a tea ceremony garden, which is bordered by a widely curved modern-style Koetsu fence. This fence and the *shihobutsu* stone basin and *oribe* stone lantern in the tea ceremony garden create an integrated view from the terrace. Extending out from the corner of the tea ceremony room to almost meet the end of the Koetsu fence is a *katsuraho* wing fence. On the east side of the front of the house is a pathway of pyroxene andesite stones. These are spaced fairly widely, with dwarf snake's beard planted in the joints to provide greenery and relatively easy management.

飯泉邸庭園
The Iizumi home garden

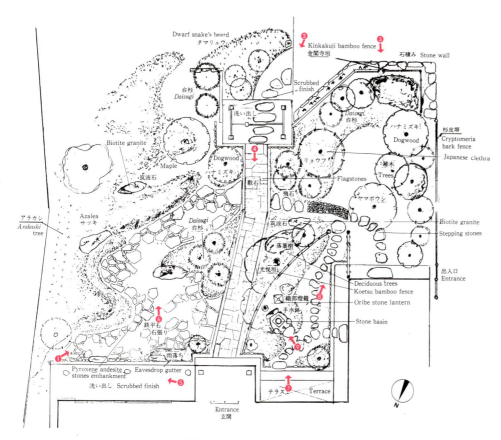

Grundrißplan   Ground plan

8. Ein *Katsuraho* Zaun erstreckt sich von der Ecke des Tee-Zeremonienraums.

7. Der Teegarten ist vom Rest des Gartens durch einen kurvigen *Koetsu* Zaun abgegrenzt.

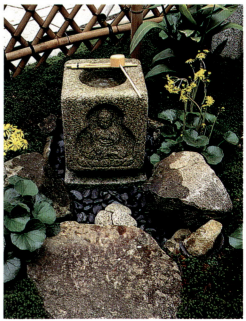

9. *Shihobutsu* Steinbecken im Teegarten.

1. Overall view of the garden. The trees in the center are Kitayama cut cryptomerias.
2. The garden gate viewed from the outside. A stone wall borders the garden on the left, while the shrubbery on the right continues into the garden.
3. The wall is of tuff in its natural state and is topped by a Kinkakuji fence.
4. The wide path from the garden gate to the house has small sections of light green andesite, providing an accent.
5. The frontage of the house to the east of the entrance. The outer border is of biotite granite; the small black stones serve as a gutter for rain from the eaves.
6. Pyroxene andesite stone pathway, with dwarf snake's beard planted in the joints.
7. The tea ceremony garden, set off from the rest of the garden by a curved Koetsu fence.
8. *Katsuraho* fence extending from the corner of the tea ceremony room.
9. *Shihobutsu* stone basin in the tea ceremony garden.

Design: Shin'ichi Kosuge (Teibo). **Construction:** Kazuo Ebihara, Hiroaki Ametani, Tatsuhiro Obuki; 1994. **Area:** 500 square meters. **Location:** Yawara, Ibaraki Pref.

西の台集会所庭園
Nishi-no-Dai Clubhouse Garden

1. Gesamtansicht des Gartens.

2. Japanische Weiß-Pinie auf der anderen Seite des Flusses.

3. Das Flußbett ist mit ovalen, flach überlappenden Steinen ausgelegt.

Das *Nishi-no-Dai* Clubhaus in eine in einer Vorstadt liegende multifunktionale Einrichtung. Es liegt auf einem nach Süden abfallenden Hang. Der als Trockenlandschaft angelegte Garten ist direkt vor dem im japanischen Stil eingerichteten Raum angelegt. Der Garten besitzt ein Arrangement eines trockenen Wasserfalls, der die Quelle zu einem trockenen Flußbett ist. Auch ein aus Steinen, Kamelien, feinen Olivenbäumen und anderen immergrünen Pflanzen erbauter Berg bringt dem Garten die nötige Tiefe. Es befinden sich auch andere Gartenpflanzen wie japanische Weiß-Pinie, Walnußbäume, *Dwarf Snake's Beard* und eine *Sasanqua* Hecke innerhalb des Zauns. Mehrere Befestigungssteine wurden gegenüber dem Flußbett als Abschluß aufgestellt und eine Uferbefestigung entlang des Flusses gebaut. Ein Teil des Flußbetts „fließt" sehr nahe am Clubhaus vorbei; hier ist die Uferbefestigung bis zum Gebäude gebaut und mit großen Ufersteinen besetzt. Andere Steinobjekte beinhalten zwei Brücken über das Flußbett, einen in den Fluß eingetauchten Stein sowie ein Grotten-Steinarrangement im flußabwärts liegenden Teil. Die Steine sind aus blauem Chlorit-Schist.

The Nishi-no-Dai Clubhouse is a suburban multi-purpose facility situated at the top of a south-facing slope. Its dry-landscape garden sits just below a Japanese-style room in the clubhouse. The garden includes a dry-waterfall stone arrangement serving as the source of a dry streambed, and a built-up mountain of stones accompanied by camellias, fragrant olives, and other evergreens, which add a sense of depth. (Other garden plants include a Japanese white pine, maples, dwarf snake's beard, and a sasanqua hedge inside the fence.) Several damlike stones have been placed across the stream for a unique effect, and embankment stone arrangements form the banks of the stream. One section of the dry streambed comes near the clubhouse; here, the bank, curving up toward the side of the building, is set with tuff, in imitation of a stony shoreline. Other stone objects include two bridges across the streambed, a stream-dividing stone, and a grotto stone arrangement in the downstream portion. The garden stones are blue chlorite-schist.

西の台集会所庭園
Nishi-no-Dai Clubhouse garden

5. Steinbrücke flußabwärts über den Fluß.

6. Der etwas tiefer gesetzte Fluß ist ein interessanter Blickfang im Garten.

4. Steinarrangement als trockener Wasserfall im Hintergrund mit der Steinbrücke gleich unterhalb des Quellensteins.

1. Overall view of the garden.
2. Japanese white pine across the stream from the clubhouse.
3. The streambed is lined with flat, oval-shaped stones arranged in an overlapping fashion to give the impression of wavelets.
4. Dry-waterfall stone arrangement in the distance, with a stone bridge just downstream from the waterfall source stone.
5. Stone bridge in the downstream section of the streambed.
6. The deep setting of the stream is an interesting feature of this garden.

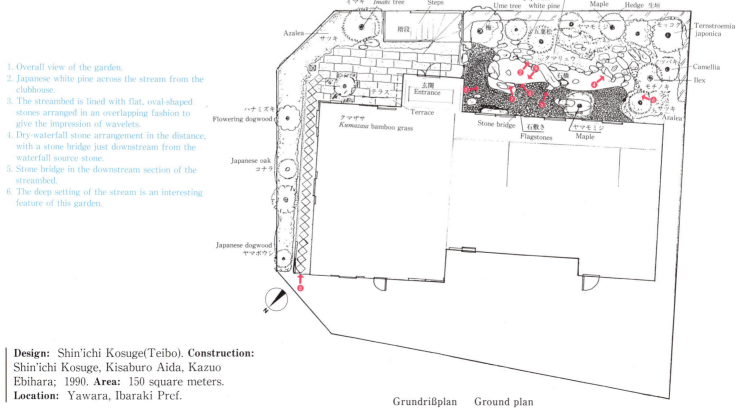

Grundrißplan   Ground plan

Design: Shin'ichi Kosuge (Teibo). **Construction:** Shin'ichi Kosuge, Kisaburo Aida, Kazuo Ebihara; 1990. **Area:** 150 square meters. **Location:** Yawara, Ibaraki Pref.

西の台集会所庭園
Nishi-no-Dai Clubhouse garden

7. Grotten-Arrangement am Ende des Flußbetts. Das Arrangement verdeckt ein Auffangbecken für Regenwasser. Der Stein links ist der größte im Garten und bringt die nötige Tiefe.

8. Ein Granit-Steinweg führt zum Parkplatz hinter dem Haus.

9. Uferbefestigung aus Steinen direkt am Clubhaus.

7. Grotto stone arrangement, at the end of the dry streambed. The arrangement serves to hide a rainwater drain. The stone on the left is the largest in the garden and helps to add depth to the garden when viewed from the clubhouse entrance.
8. Granite flagstone path leading from the front of the clubhouse to the parking area in the back.
9. Stony-shoreline appearance of the stream bank near the side of the clubhouse.

高橋邸庭園
The Takahashi Home Garden

1. Der Weg führt zum Vordereingang des Hauses. Das Haarmoos und die verschiedenen Bäume schaffen einen außerirdischen Eindruck.

2. Traditionelles Tor und der davorliegende Parkplatz.

3. Gebogener *Koetsu* Zaun neben dem Hauseingang.

4. Große unregelmäßig geformte hellgrüne *Andesite* Steine sind zu einem Fußweg zusammengetragen worden. Die Bodenbepflanzung ist Haarmoos.

1. The pathway leading to the front entrance of the house. The hair moss and various trees create an otherworldly impression.
2. Traditional gate and parking area outside it.
3. Curved Koetsu fence near the entrance to the house.
4. Large, irregular light green andesite stones were arranged to form an interesting pathway. The ground cover is hair moss.

高橋邸庭園
The Takahashi home garden

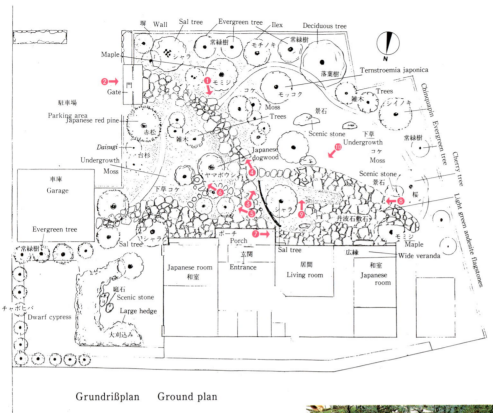

Grundrißplan   Ground plan

5. Im *Kitayama* Stil geschnittene *Cryptomeria*.

5. Kitayama cut cryptomerias near the house entrance.
6. Coin-shaped stone basin in front of the house.
7. *Katsuraho* fence on the porch outside the house entrance.
8. Terrace of light green andesite stones inside the garden. The trees of the main garden are spread out, in contrast to the grovelike effect of the front garden.
9. This Japanese red pine stands out well in the small grassy area in the center of the garden.
10. Koetsu fence dividing the main and front gardens.

6. Steinbecken im Münzenform vor dem Haus.

7. *Katsuraho* Zaun, um die Terrasse am Haus gezogen.

Der Garten des *Takahashi Homes* ist auf der Südseite des Hauses; eine Straße mit einer Garage befindet sich östlich des Hauses. Zuerst wurden die Positionen der Bäume festgelegt. Auch das Tor und die Mauer sollten in dem relativ großen Garten ihren Platz bekommen. Das Ergebnis ist ein sehr schön ausgewogener Garten, der mit den Strukturen des Hauses harmoniert. Der Garten kann in einen nach Osten ausgerichteten, mit vielen Bäumen versehenen Vorgarten sowie einen auf dem restlichen Grundstück verteilten Hauptgarten eingeteilt werden. Die Gärten sind durch einen Bambuszaun im südlichen Teil und eine Ziegelmauer getrennt. Der Vorgarten ist mit vielen Bäumen und Büschen wie Azaleen, japanischen Rot-Pinien, Walnußbäumen und im *Kitayama* Stil geschnittene *Cryptomeria* bepflanzt. Der Boden ist mit Haarmoos bepflanzt und macht den vom Außentor zum Haus führenden Weg interessanter. Die Steine sind hellgrüne *Andesite,* die in unregelmäßige, verschieden große Stücke geschnitten sind. Auch zwischen den Steinen wächst Haarmoos.

Die leicht gekurvte Terrasse im Hauptgarten ist ebenfalls aus hellgrüner *Andesite*. Auch hier wurde Haarmoos in die leichten Kurven gepflanzt. Der Hauptgarten erscheint durch seinen hügeligen Rasen und den Bäumen (japanischen Rot-Pinien, Pflaumenbäumen, kleinen Olivenbäumen und Walnußbäumen) sehr groß.

The garden of the Takahashi home is on the south side of the house, and there is a driveway and garage to the east of the garden. We first purchased a number of trees, and "eyeballed" appropriate positions for them, as well as for the gate and walls, in the relatively large garden. The result is a well-integrated layout among the garden and the structures on the property.

The garden can be divided into a front garden, facing the eastern half of the house and containing numerous trees, and a main garden on the rest of the property; the two are divided by a bamboo screen fence in the south part of the garden and tiled wall. The front garden has numerous trees and shrubs, including azaleas, Japanese red pines, maples, and Kitayama cut cryptomeria. Covered with hair moss, the ground undulates somewhat, adding interest to the path that leads from the outer gate to the entrance to the house. The stones of the path are of light green andesite, cut irregularly into large pieces; hair moss is planted between the stones as well.

Light green andesite stone are laid out in a curved terrace in the main garden, with a small mound of hair moss inside the curve. The main garden appears expansive, with its hilly lawn and Japanese red pines, plum trees, fragrant olives, and maples.

高橋邸庭園
The Takahashi home garden

8. Terrasse aus hellgrüner *Andesite* im Garten. Die Bäume im Hauptgarten sind gut verteilt. Im Gegensatz zum Hain im Vorgarten.

9. Die japanische Rot-Pinie paßt sehr gut in die Mitte des schmalen grasigen Gartens.

10. Ein *Koetsu* Zaun ziert den Haupt- und Vorgarten.

Design: Shin'ichi Kosuge(Teibo). **Construction:** Shin'ichi Kosuge, Kazuo Ebihara, Yoshikazu; 1992. **Area:** 900 square meters. **Location:** Tsukuba, Ibaraki Pref.

Glossar

Bemerkung: Für weitere Informationen bezüglich der folgenden Punkte verweisen wir Sie auf nachstehende Bücher, die alle von Graphic-sha veröffentlicht wurden.

Bambuszäune: *Osamu Suzuki* und *Isao Yoshikawa,* Japans Bambuszäune (1988).
Steinbecken: *Isao Yoshikawa,* Steinbecken (1988).
Ziersteine: *Isao Yoshikawa,* Japanische Stein-Gärten: Bedeutung und Gestaltung (1992).

Geschichtsperioden

Nara: 645–794
Heian: 794–1185
Kamakura: 1185–1333
Muromachi: 1333–1573
Momoyama: 1573–1603
Edo/Tokugawa: 1603–1868
Meiji: 1868–1912

Begriffe

Agesudo: Ein hängendes *Shiorido,* das durch erhöhten Grund und Mittelpunkt gehalten wird.

Amida: (Skt. Amitabha): Der Lord des „Pure Land" (Paradies) im Westen, Mitglied der „Pure Land" Buddhisten-Sekten. Er wird als Retter der Erde angesehen.

Außengarten: Der Teil des Tee-Zeremoniengartens, in dem die Gäste den Gastgeber erwarten.

Blaustein: Überbegriff für Steine mit grüner oder blauer Färbung, meist Chlorit-Schist. Sie wurden vornehmlich während der *Muromachi* Periode für Gärten im Stil von indischen Tintengemälden verwendet.

Carp-Stein: Ein Stein im Wasserfall-Steinarrangement. Er stellt eine Vertiefung dar, aus der das Wasser fällt.

Cryptomeria im Kitayama-Stil geschnitten: Ein *Cryptomeria* Baum, dessen Stamm in 50 m Höhe abgeschnitten ist; jetzt können neue Blätter nachwachsen.

Empfangszimmer: Ein kleines Gebäude (meist im Außengarten), in dem die Gäste den Gastgeber erwarten.

-en: Garten *(suffix).*

Erbauter Hügel (Berg etc.): Ein kunstvoll erbauter Hügel im Garten; oft sind Steinarrangements darauf plaziert.

Flügelstein: Ein Stein, der den Flügel in einem Kranich- oder Kranichinsel-Steinarrangement darstellt.

Flügelzaun: Ein hoher Zaun neben einem Gebäude, der meist als Sichtschutzzaun dient.

Flußstein: Ein Stein, der ein Stück flußabwärts des Wasserfalls plaziert wird und die Wassermassen teilt.

Garten als trockene Landschaft: Ein Garten, der keine Wasserkörper enthält (obwohl er diese widerspiegeln soll, z.B. trockenes Flußbett, trockene Wasserfälle und trockene Teiche).

Garten im Stil eines indischen Tinten-Gemäldes: Ein nach einem chinesischen oder japanischen Gemälde aus indischer Tinte angelegter Garten.

Hokyointo: Eine Stein *Stupa* mit quadratischer Basis und quadratischem Körper. Das Dach ist treppenförmig gelegt mit einem *Sorin* (ringförmige Zierspitze).

Horai **Insel:** Eine Insel analog zu *Mt. Horai* (q.v.); man sagt, er steht auf dem Rücken einer riesigen Schildkröte. Früher verwendeten Gärtner *Horai* Inseln als ein Symbol der Langlebigkeit.

Horai **Steinarrangement:** Ein Überbegriff für verschiedene Arrangements, alle mit bestimmten Bedeutungen, angelehnt an die *Mt. Horai* Legende (q.v.). Sie enthalten Kranich- und Schildkröten-Arrangements.

Innengarten: Der innere Teil des Tee-Zeremoniengartens mit Tee-Zeremonienhaus.

Innentor: Das Tor trennt den inneren und äußeren Garten vom Tee-Zeremoniengarten.

-ji: Tempel *(suffix).*

Kannon: (Skt. Avalokiteshvara): Ein Bodhisattva, der die Personifizierung von Mitleid und Gnade zusammen mit Buddha Amida, dem Retter der Erde, darstellt.

Kasa **Steinbecken:** Ein Steinbecken aus einem umgedrehten Dachziegel *(kasa)* von *Stupas* und anderen Stein-Monumenten.

Kesa **Steinbecken:** Ein Becken aus einem zylinder- oder faßförmigen Teil eines Hoto (eine Art *Stupa*). Ein *Kesa* ist ein Behälter eines Buddhisten-Priesters, die diesen Becken ähneln sollen.

Kranichhals-Stein: Ein langer Stein, der den Hals des Kranichs darstellt. Stein „Entfernter Hügel": Ein bergförmiger Stein (z.B. neben einem Wasserfall aufgestellt), der die nötige Perspektive und Tiefe im Garten erzeugt.

Kranichinsel-Steinarrangement (Kranichinsel): Ein Kranich-Steinarrangement in einem Gartenteich als Insel gebaut.

Kranich-Steinarrangement: Ein Arrangement in Form eines Kranichs, meist ziemlich abstrakt; der Kranich ist ein Symbol orientalischer Traditionen (z.B. *Horai* Steinarrangement).

Lamellen-Fenster: Ein quadratisches Fenster in einer gemauerten Wand (z.B. in einem *Sukiya* Tor oder einer Tee-Zeremonienstruktur), das beim Erbauen freigelassen wurde und mit Bambus oder Holzlamellen ausgekleidet ist.

Moso **Bambus:** Eine dickstämmige Bambusart; *Phyllostachys* pubescens.

Mount Horai: Ein Berg in einer chinesischen Sage, auf dem uralte Wizzards lebten; er symbolisiert Langlebigkeit.

Rendai **Steinbecken:** Ein aus dem Sockel *(rendai)* einer Buddha-Statue oder aus einer *Stupa* gemachtes Becken; „ren" bezieht sich auf den Lotusblüten, die in solche Sockel graviert wurden.

Ryumonbaku: Ein Wasserfallarrangement, nach dem „Drachentor-Wasserfall" benannt, einer Stromschnelle im Gelben Fluß in China; das Arrangement enthält einen Carp Stein als Basis, der das Wasser vor dem „Fall" sammelt.

Sanzon **Steinarrangement:** Ein Arrangement aus drei Steinen, das nach den drei Hauptfiguren in der Gebetshalle eines Buddhisten-Tempel benannt ist: ein Buddha in der Mitte und ein Bodhisattva an jeder Seite.

Schildkröteninsel-Steinarrangement (Schildkröteninsel): Ein Schildkröteninsel-Arrangement als Insel in einem Teich positioniert (siehe *Horai* Insel).

Schildkrötenkopf-Stein: Ein Stein, der den Kopf der Schildkröte in einem

Schildkröten-Arrangement oder einer Schildkröteninsel darstellt.

Schildkröten-Steinarrangement: Ein in Form einer Schildkröte angelegtes Arrangement – ein überliefertes Symbol orientalischer Traditionen (siehe *Horai* Steinarrangement).

***Shihobutsu* Steinbecken:** Ein aus einer vierseitigen *Stupa* gemachtes Becken, das auf jeder Seite eine Buddha-Zeichnung hat *(shihobutsu)*.

Shiorido: Ein Gartenzaun aus einem viereckigen Bambusrahmen, um den dünnen Bambusstreifen gezogen sind. Dabei entsteht ein rautenförmiges Netz.

Shishiodoshi: Ein Bambusrohr, das sich mit Wasser füllt und sich dann auf einen Stein tropfend entleert; dabei entsteht ein Echo.

Spiral-Steinarrangement: Ein Arrangement aus zahlreichen Steinen, die um einen Mittelstein spiralenförmig ausgelegt sind.

Stehendes Steinbecken: Ein relativ hohes Steinbecken, bei dem sich der Besucher nicht bücken muß, um Wasser zu schöpfen; es unterscheidet sich von einem Verandabecken vor allem, daß es vom Haus entfernt steht.

Steinarrangement: Ein Arrangement aus zwei oder mehr Steinen, die einen ausdruckstarken Effekt erzielen (auch ein einziger Stein kann als Arrangement betrachtet werden).

Steinbecken *(J., chozubachi)*: Ein Becken, das Wasser für rituelle Gesten enthält (z.B. zum Händewaschen; um den Mund vor Tee-Zeremonien auszuspülen – symbolisch reinigt dies den Geist). *Chozubachi* kann aus Keramik, Holz, Metall und aus Stein sein. In manchen Gärten dienen sie auch nur zur Zierde.

Steinlaterne: In diesem Buch steht der Begriff für viele verschiedene Steinlaternen, waren ursprünglich in Schreinen und Tempeln aufgestellt. Sie stehen immer für sich allein. Die meisten Laternengehäuse sind sechs- oder achteckig, obwohl auch vier- oder dreieckige und runde Formen existieren. Steinlaternen wurden während der *Momoyama* Periode in Tee-Zeremoniengärten aufgestellt. In dieser Zeit entstanden auch viele andere Formen. Eine „*Oki-Doro*" (kleine Steinlaterne) ist eine spezielle Form ohne Sockel und Abdeckung, die auf ein Podest gestellt wird (die meisten der im Buch aufgeführten Laternen werden im Glossar nicht gesondert erwähnt, da sie durch ihre Form und Photos sehr schön zur Geltung kommen).

Steinlaterne im Sode-Stil: Eine aus einem quadratischen Steinquader gemachte Laterne, in die eine rechteckige Kerbe für die Flamme geschnitten wurde; es entsteht eine C-Form.

Suikinkutsu: Ein kleiner unterirdischer Raum an einem Steinbecken oder *Tsukubai*, in den Wassertropfen fallen und somit ein Echo erzeugen.

-*tei:* Inn, Restaurant *(suffix)*.

-*tei:* Garten *(suffix)*.

***Teppatsu* Steinbecken:** Ein Steinbecken in Form einer Bettelschale eines Mendicanten-Priesters.

Treppenstein: Ein neben die Veranda oder den Eingang gelegter Stein, auf den die Schuhe gestellt werden, bevor man das Haus betritt.

Tsukubai: Ein Steinarrangement mit Steinbecken *(chozubachi)* in der Mitte. Die Steine bestehen aus einem Vorderstein, auf den sich die Gäste knien, um Wasser zu schöpfen; außerdem gehören ein Stein für heißes Wasser (für den Gebrauch im Winter) und ein Kerzenstein (für nächtliche Tee-Zeremonien) zu dem Arrangement.

Veranda-Steinbecken: Ein großes Steinbecken direkt unterhalb der Verdanda eines Hauses. Es kann sowohl neben dem Badezimmer als auch am Tee-Zeremoniengarten stehen. Manchmal steht es aber auch nur zur Zierde irgendwo im Garten. Quellenstein eines Wasserfalls: der Stein an der Spitze des Wasserfalls, von dem das Wasser tropft.

Waschbeton: Steht für zwei verschiedene Oberflächen (auf Wegen oder Wänden), die vor dem Trocknen geschruppt oder gewaschen werden: a) eine Betonoberfläche, in die mit einer Bürste oder einem anderen Gegenstand Muster eingeritzt werden; b) eine Mörteloberfläche, in die Granitstücke, Marmor oder andere Steinstücke eingebracht werden, bevor er vollkommen trocken ist.

Wellenstein: Ein Stein mitten im Gartenteich, der so gestellt ist, daß er das Wasser im Teich Wellen schlagen läßt.

***Yin-Yang* Stein:** Ein Stein, der weibliche und männliche Genitalien darstellt und somit Fruchtbarkeit symbolisiert. Solche Steine wurden oft in Daimyo-Gärten der frühen *Edo* Periode aufgestellt.

***Zazen* Stein:** Ein abgeflachter Stein, der möglicherweise für *Zen*-Meditation verwendet wurde.

Glossary

Note: For further details on the following topics, please consult the following books, all published by Graphic-sha.

Bamboo fences: Osamu Suzuki and Isao Yoshikawa, *The Bamboo Fences of Japan* (1988).
Garden stones: Isao Yoshikawa, *Japanese Stone Gardens: Appreciation and Creation* (1992).
Stone basins: Isao Yoshikawa, *Stone Basins* (1988).

Historical Periods

Nara: 645–794
Heian: 794–1185
Kamakura: 1185–1333
Muromachi: 1333–1573
Momoyama: 1573–1603
Edo/Tokugawa: 1603–1868
Meiji: 1868–1912

Terms

agesudo: A hanging *shiorido* held open by raising up the bottom and holding it in place with a pole.
Amida (Skt., Amitabha): The lord of the Pure Land (paradise) in the west, worshipped in the Pure Land sects of Buddhism and viewed as the savior of the world.
blue stone: General term for stones that are green or blue in color, usually chlorite-schist. They were used frequently during the Muromachi period in gardens laid out in the india ink painting style.
built-up hill (mountain, etc.): An artificially built-up mound in a garden; stone arrangements are often placed on it.
carp stone: A stone in a waterfall stone arrangement representative of a carp attempting to ascend the waterfall.
crane island stone arrangement (crane island): A crane stone arrangement positioned as an island in a garden pond.
crane stone arrangement: A stone arrangement made to resemble a crane, usually rather abstractly; the crane is an auspicious symbol in Oriental tradition (*see* Horai stone arrangement).
crane's neck stone: A long stone representative of a crane's neck in crane and crane island stone arrangements.
distant-mountain stone: A mountain-shaped or similar stone placed in a garden (near a waterfall, for example) in such a way as to create a sense of perspective and depth.
dry-landscape garden: A garden that includes no bodies of water in it (although it may have representations of these, such as dry streambeds, dry waterfalls, and dry ponds).
-en: Garden (suffix).
hokyointo: A stone stupa with a square base, a square body, a roof with a steplike structure, and a *sorin* (ringed decorative spire) at the top.
Horai Island: An island analogous to Mount Horai (*q.v.*); it is said to have been located on the back of a huge turtle. Ancient gardeners included Horai Islands in their gardens as symbols of longevity.
Horai stone arrangement: A general term for various arrangements, all of them with auspicious associations, related to the Mount Horai (*q.v.*) legend, including crane and turtle stone arrangements.
india ink painting-style garden: A garden laid out in imitation of old Chinese and Japanese landscape paintings done in india ink.
inner garden: The inner section of a tea ceremony garden, containing the tea ceremony house.
inner gate: The gate separating the inner and outer gardens of a tea ceremony garden.
-ji: Temple (suffix).
Kannon (Skt., Avalokiteshvara): A bodhisattva who is considered the personification of compassion and mercy and, along with the buddha Amida, the savior of the world.
kasa **stone basin**: A basin made from the "roof" (*kasa*) section, used upside-down, of stupas and other stone monuments.
kesa **stone basin**: A basin made from the cylinder- or barrel-shaped portion of *hoto*, a type of stupa. A *kesa* is Buddhist priest's surplice, which these basins are said to resemble.
Kitayama cut cryptomeria: A cryptomeria tree whose trunk is cut off at about 50 meters from ground level; new leaves are allowed to bud at the cut.
lathwork window: A window in a wall (usually of a Sukiya gate or tea ceremony structure) that is made by simply not plastering over a square of the wall as the wall is being made; the bamboo or wooden laths (i.e., groundwork) of the wall are thus exposed.
moso **bamboo**: A species of thick-stemmed bamboo; *Phyllostachys pubescens*.
Mount Horai: A mountain in Chinese folklore on which ageless wizards lived; it symbolizes longevity.
outer garden: The outer section of a tea ceremony garden, where the guests await the host.
reception hut: A small building in a tea ceremony garden (usually the outer garden) where guests await the host before proceeding.
rendai **stone basin**: A basin made from the pedestal (*rendai*) of a statue of the Buddha or a stupa; "ren" refers to the lotus petals carved into such pedestals.
ryumonbaku: A waterfall arrangement named after the "dragon gate waterfall," a rapid section of the Yellow River in China; the arrangement contains a carp stone at the base, which abstractly represents a carp attempting to ascend the falls.
sanzon **stone arrangement**: An arrangement of three stones patterned after the three main figures in the worship hall of a Buddhist temple: a buddha in the center and a bodhisattva on either side.
scrubbed finish: Refers to two types of surfaces (pavements, walls, etc.) that are scrubbed and washed before the material dries: (*a*) a concrete surface in which the concrete is scraped over with a wire brush or other implement before it is completely dry; (*b*) a mortar surface in which the pieces of granite, marble, or other stone mixed in with the mortar are exposed by washing away the surface mortar before it is dry.
shihobutsu **stone basin**: A basin made from the body of a four-sided stupa that has a carving of the Buddha on each side (an object known as a *shihobutsu*).
shiorido: A garden wicket made of a

square frame of bamboo around which are stretched thin strips of bamboo sheathed in such a way as to form a rhombus-shaped mesh.

shishiodoshi: A bamboo device that filled with is and releases water, making an echoing sound against a rock as it drops back to position.

sode-style stone lantern: A lantern made of a square column of stones with a rectangular notch cut out of it for the flame; the result is a C shape.

spiral stone arrangement: A stone arrangement of numerous stones positioned around a large central stone in a spiral layout.

standing stone basin: A relatively tall basin that does not require the visitor to stoop down to get water; it differs from a veranda stone basin in that it is located away from a building.

step-up stone: A stone placed near a veranda or entrance and used for removing footwear before stepping up into the house.

stone arrangement: An arrangement of two or more stones selected and positioned for expressive effect. (A single stone so positioned may also be considered a stone arrangement.)

stone basin (J., *chozubachi*): A basin holding water for ritual ablutions (e.g., for washing the hands and rinsing out the mouth prior to the tea ceremony symbolizing the purification of the spirit). *Chozubachi* may be made of ceramic, wood, and metal, as well as stone. In some gardens, they often serve a decorative purpose only.

stone lantern: In this book, the term refers to the various types of stone lanterns used originally in shrines and temples. They were originally used singly, then in pairs. Most lantern bases and columns are hexagonal or octagonal, although square, triangular, and round ones exist. Stone lanterns came to be used freely in tea ceremony gardens during the Momoyama period, at which time a greater variety of styles became evident. An *oki-doro* (called a "small stone lantern" in this book) is a special type in which the body of the lantern, without a base and column, is placed on a pedestal. (Most of the specific types of stone lanterns mentioned in this book are not defined separately in this glossary, since they are most easily "defined" by their shapes, as seen in the photographs.)

stream-dividing stone: A stone placed somewhat downstream from a garden waterfall, to split the water flow as it passes the stone.

suikinkutsu: A small underground chamber near a stone basin or tsukubai in which water droplets are allowed to fall and echo.

-tei: Inn, restaurant (suffix).

-tei: Garden (suffix).

teppatsu **stone basin**: A stone basin in the shape of a mendicant priest's begging bowl.

tsukubai: A stone arrangement with a stone basin (*chozubachi*) at its center. The stones include a *front stone*, which guests stoop on in order to get water from the basin; a *hot-water bucket* stone, for use in winter; and a *candlestick stone*, for tea ceremonies held at night.

turtle head stone: A stone representative of a turtle's head in a turtle or turtle island stone arrangement.

turtle island stone arrangement (turtle island): A turtle stone arrangement positioned as an island in a garden pond (*see* Horai island).

turtle stone arrangement: A stone arrangement made to resemble a turtle, an auspicious symbol in Oriental tradition (*see* Horai stone arrangement).

veranda stone basin: A tall stone basin directly accessible from the veranda of a house. It may be located near a lavatory or tea ceremony room, or may be just decorative.

waterfall source stone: The stone at the top of an artificial waterfall from which the water drops.

wave-dividing stone: A stone in the middle of a garden pond, placed in such a way that it appears to be splitting the waves in the body of water.

wing fence: A tall, narrow fence attached to the side of a building, usually for screening purposes.

wing stone: A stone representative of a wing in crane and crane island stone arrangements.

yin-yang stone: A stone representing the male and female genitals and thus symbolizing fertility. Such stones were used frequently in the gardens of the daimyo during the early Edo period.

zazen stone: A flat-topped stone, possibly used originally for Zen meditation.

吉河 功（よしかわ　いさお）

1940年東京生まれ。芝浦工業大学建築科卒。1963年，日本庭園研究会を創立。現在同会会長。吉河功庭園研究室代表。中国蘇州市風景園林学会名誉理事，中国杭州市風景園林学会名誉理事。日本庭園研究家，作庭家，石造美術品設計家，等として活躍している。

主要著作に『竹垣』(1977，有明書房)，『日本の名園手法』(1978年，建築資料研究社)，『造園細部資料集』(1978年，建築資料研究社)，『敷石・飛石』(1979年，有明書房)，『京の庭』(1981年，講談社)，『竹垣・石組図解事典』(1984年，建築資料研究社)，『日本庭園人物誌』(1993年，日本庭園研究会)。
グラフィック社からは『竹垣のデザイン』(1988年，共著)，『手水鉢』(1989年)，『中国江南の名園』(1990年)，『庭・エクステリア』(1990年)，『禅寺の庭』(1991年)，『石組の庭』(1992年)，を出版している。

住所　東京都世田谷区赤堤2-30-4　〒156
TEL・FAX　03-3322-7407

三橋一夫（みつはし　かずお）

1941年千葉生れ。明治大学卒。
1970年日本庭園研究会会長吉河功氏に師事。
1975年㈱三橋庭園設計事務所を設立し，新しい感覚で，デザイン性のある庭園，ランドスケープに取り組み，海外との交流も盛んに行う作庭家として活躍している。

日本庭園研究会理事，日本庭園協会理事，日本庭園学会理事の職にあり，日本庭園協会に於て，若手造園家育成のための「伝統庭園技塾」の企画，運営，講師を務めている。
主要著作に『わが家の庭づくり』(1984年，主婦と生活社)，『新感覚の住いの庭』(1989，講談社，共著)，『庭のデザイン実例集』(1991，家の光協会)，『住宅用，植栽マニュアル』(1994，建築知識社，共著)を出版している。

住所　千葉市花見川区作新台6-5-1　〒262
TEL　043-257-1299　FAX043-257-6165

曽根三郎（そね　さぶろう）

1946年大阪生まれ。大阪府立園芸高校卒業後，京都大学農学部林学科造園教室にて研究。1967年研修生として渡米。ワシントン州エベレットコミュニティカレッジにて造園学を学び，オレゴン州にて造園工事を行う。1971年樋口造園株式会社の総括責任者として，宮内庁，金閣寺，銀閣寺，北野天満宮，泉涌寺等の造園事業を行う。1976年曽根造園設立開業。東大寺，宮内庁，天龍寺，東福寺御用達となり，現在は株式会社日本造園技術研究所・匠豊丸，有限会社曽根造園の両代表取締役社長。古庭園の管理経験を生かして，文化財庭園の修復復元や作庭とに海外・国内で活躍している。日本造園組合連合会・花博指導員。日本造園組合連合会で講演会活動。第1回庭園設計表現コンクール・建設省都市局長賞。第2回庭園設計表現コンクール・労働大臣賞(第1位)。第3回庭園設計表現コンクール・労働大臣賞(第1位)。国際花と緑の博覧会・京都府スポットガーデン設計コンペ第1位。第11回全国都市緑化きょうとフェア・ランドスケープ花壇の部で奨励賞，日本庭園協会賞受賞。樹木医。1995年5月，急逝。

連絡先　京都市北区大北山原谷乾町255-6　〒603
TEL　075-462-6058　FAX　075-463-5526

小菅新一（こすげ　しんいち）

1952年，茨城県生まれ。茨城県立取手第一高等学校園芸科卒業。
1970年，株式会社川上農場造園部入社。川上農場創立者・川上三郎氏に師事し，日本庭園の美に興味をもつ。
1976年，日本庭園研究会に入会。以後，日本庭園研究会の例会・研修会などで庭園史・庭園美学などについて学ぶ。
1981年，川上農場退社。「庭房小管」として独立し，現在に至る。

住所　茨城県筑波郡谷和原村寺畑336-1　〒300-24
TEL　0297-52-4615

日本庭園研究会について

日本庭園研究会【略称・庭研】は，一般愛庭家，作庭家を問わず，研究の促進と，親睦を目的として，庭園を愛するすべての人々に開放されている研究団体。1995年現在すでに30年以上の実績を持っている。同会では年数回の実地研修会，月一度の研究会等を通して，幅広い活動を展開している。また年6回，会誌『庭研』を発行し会員に配布しており，同誌はすでに300号に達している（費用は，入会金5,000　年間維持費15,000）。お問い合せは庭研本部（〒156 東京都世田谷区赤堤2-30-4／TEL・FAX 03-3322-7407）へ。

Das Japanische Gartenforschungsinstitut ist eine für alle Liebhaber japanischer Gärten offene Forschergruppe. Das Japanische Gartenforschungsinstitut hat es sich zur Aufgabe gemacht, die alten Traditionen zu fördern. Nun, 1995, besteht es schon seit über dreißig Jahren. Es führt regelmäßig Untersuchungen und Studien durch, hält einmal im Monat eine Forschungs-Konferenz ab und veröffentlicht zweimal im Monat das Journal „Garden Studies" (Teiken), das an die Mitglieder herausgegeben wird und schon seine 300ste Auflage erreicht hat. Die in diesem Buch veröffentlichten Arbeiten stammen von Mitgliedern dieses Instituts.

Isao Yoshikawa wurde 1940 geboren und studierte im technischen College in Shibaura. Er gründete 1963 das Japanische Gartenforschungsinstitut und ist nun sein Präsident. Des weiteren ist er Mitglied der Japanischen Gartengesellschaft, Präsident der Soshu Chinese Gartengesellschaft und der Koshu Chinese Gartengesellschaft. Er erforscht japanische Gärten, ist Gartengestaltungskünstler und Bildhauer. Seine veröffentlichten Werke sind Methods of Famous Japanese Gardes, A Reference for Japanese Garden Elements, An Illustrated Dictionary of Bamboo Fences and Stone Walls, Gardens of Kyoto sowie die im Graphic-sha Verlag erschienenen The Bamboo Fences of Japan (Takegaki no Dezain), a collaborative work, Stone Basins Chinese Gardens, Elements of Japanese Gardens and The World of Zen Gardens and Japanese Stone Gardens.

Kazuo Mitsuhashi wurde 1941 geboren und studierte an der Meiji Universität. 1975 eröffnete er das Mitsuhashi Gartenplanungs-Büro. Sein Ziel war es, frische neue Ideen in das Gartendesign aufzunehmen. Er arbeitete sehr viel für Kunden aus Übersee. Er war Präsident der Japanischen Landschaftsgesellschaft, des Japanischen Gartenforschungsinstituts und der Japanischen Gartenvereinigung. Seine veröffentlichten Werke sind Garden-Building for the Home, Gardens for a New Kind of Dwelling, Works of Garden Design und Garden Plants for the Home.

Saburo Sone wurde 1946 geboren. Nachdem er die City High School Garden Arts Department in Osaka abgeschlossen hatte, studierte er an der Universität für Landwirtschaft und Garten in Kyoto. 1967 bereiste er die USA als Austauschstudent und schrieb sich im Everett Community College für Landschaftsarchitektur ein. 1971 wurde er Geschäftsführer der Hisuchi Noen Corp. und war Projektleiter für das Imperial Palace, den Tempel des Goldenen Pavillons, den Tempel des Silbernen Pavillons und den Kitano Tenman Palast. Seit er 1976 die Stone Garden Planning Co. gründete, ist er für Gartenrestauration und Bauprojekte in nationalen Denkmälern wie dem Todai-ji Tempel, Imperial Palace, Tenryu-ji Tempel und Tofuku-ji Tempel zuständig. Ebenso betreut er Projekte in Übersee. Seine Referenzen sind die Präsidentschaften der Japanischen Landschaftsgesellschaft, der Japanischen Gartenvereinigung, der Japanischen Gartenakademie und des Japanischen Gartenforschungsinstituts.

Shin'ichi Kosuge wurde 1952 geboren und studierte an der High School für Gartenbaukunst in der Ibaraki Präfektur. Er besuchte die Landschaftsbauschule der Kawakami Farm und erlernte die japanische Gartenbaukunst durch den Gründer dieser Schule, Herrn Kawakami Saburo. 1976 trat er in die Japanische Gartenforschungsgesellschaft ein und erweiterte seine Studien in speziellen Treffen und Seminaren der Gesellschaft. 1981 verließ er dann die Kawakami Farm und gründete seine Firma – Kosuge Garden Studio.

Japanese Garden Research Association is a research group open to all lovers of the Japanese garden, regardless of profession, and seeks only to promote the appreciation of the tradtition. As of 1995, it has been in existence for more than thirty years, and today undertakes several specific survey projects each year, holds monthly research conferences, and publishes a bimonthly journal, „Garden Studies" (Teiken), which is circulated among its members and has reached its 300th issue. The works introduced in this book are all by members of the Association.

Isao Yoshikawa was born in 1940, and graduated from Shibaura Technical College. He founded the Japanese Garden Research Association in 1963, and is now its chairman. He is also active as a member of the Japanese Garden Society, chairman of the Soshu Chinese Garden Society, and the Koshu Chinese Garden Society, Japanese garden researcher, garden artist and rock carver. His published works include Methods of Famous Japanese Gardens, A Reference for Japanese Garden Elements, An Illustrated Dictionary of Bamboo Fences and Stone Walls, Gardens of Kyoto, and with Grapfic-sha, The Bamboo Fences of Japan (Takegaki no Dezain), a collaborative work, Stone Basins Chinese Gardens, Elements of Japanese Gardens and The World of Zen Gardens andJapanese Stone Gardens.

Kazuo Mitsuhashi was born in 1941, and graduated form Meiji University. In 1975 he established Mitsuhashi Garden Planning Office, with the aim of promoting fresh feelings and ideas for garden design, and has worked frequently clients overseas. He has acted as the chairman of the Japanese Landscape Society, Japanese Garden Research Association, and the Japanese Garden Association. His works include Garden-Building for the Home, Gardens for a New Kind of Dwelling, Works of Garden Design, and Garden Plants for the Home.

Saburo Sone was born in 1946, and after graduating from Osaka City High School Garden Arts Department, studied in the Garden Department of Kyoto University's Agricultural School. In 1967 he visited the U.S. as a research student, enrolling in Everett Community College's Landscape Department. In 1971 he became the chief of Higuchi Noen Corp., and took responsibility for garden projects at the Imerpial Palace, Temple of the Golden Pavilion, Temple of the Silver Pavilion, and the Kitano Tenman Palace. Since establishing Stone Garden Planning Co., in 1976, he has been responsible for garden restorations and construction projects at such national treasures as Todai-ji Temple, Imperial Palace, Tenryu-ji Temple and Tofuku-ji Temple, as well as other projects both in Japan and overseas. His appointments have included chairmanship of the Japanese Landscape Society, Japanese Garden Association, Japanese Garden Academy and Japanese Garden Research Association.

Shin'ichi Kosuge was born in 1952, and graduated from Ibaraki Prefectural High School's Gardening Arts Department. He joined Kawakami Farm's Landscaping Department and gained an appreciation of the Japanese garden under the tutelage of company founder, Kawakami Saburo. In 1976, he joined the Japanese Garden Research Society, and continued his studies of the Japanese garden at special meetings and seminars of the Society. In 1981, he quit Kawakami Farms, and established his present company, Kosuge Garden Studio.